Tableau Desktop Specialist Certification

A prep guide with multiple learning styles to help you gain
Tableau Desktop Specialist certification

Adam Mico

BIRMINGHAM—MUMBAI

Tableau Desktop Specialist Certification

Publishing Product Manager: Apeksha Shetty
Senior Editor: Tazeen Shaikh
Technical Editor: Kavyashree K S
Copy Editor: Safis Editing
Project Coordinator: Farheen Fathima
Proofreader: Safis Editing
Indexer: Hemangini Bari
Production Designer: Vijay Kamble
Marketing Coordinators: Nivedita Singh

First published: January 2023
Production reference: 1310123

Published by Packt Publishing Ltd.
Livery Place
35 Livery Street
Birmingham
B3 2PB, UK.

ISBN 978-1-80181-013-5

www.packtpub.com

To the #DataFam, which includes the Tableau community and supportive people of Team Tableau, who have inspired me to find my voice and to bet on myself. You have changed my life immeasurably. To my original mentor, Amy Banicki, who enabled me to change courses in my career and helped expose me to Tableau. To my patient wife, Kristina, who has always encouraged and supported me with stability. To my son, Addisson, who has become his own incredible man, husband, and father. And finally, my granddaughter, Madeline, who came into the world on February 22, 2022.

– Adam Mico

Contributors

About the author

Adam Mico is the principal, data visualization and enablement at Moderna. Before that, he worked as a Tableau evangelist for Keyrus US. He is a two-time Michael W. Cristiani Community Leadership Award winner (Tableau Conference). He is also a Tableau visionary, mentor, Tableau Speaker Bureau member, and a Tableau ambassador. In his free time, he enjoys traveling, finding the next great bite, and spending time with his family and dog.

About the reviewers

Maulik Vyas is currently a BI analyst at TD Bank, one of the leading banks in North America, working in a data visualization and advanced analytics team. He holds a master's degree in electrical and computer engineering from the University of Windsor. He has several years of experience working on projects involving Tableau. He passed the Tableau Desktop Specialist test with a 95% score. In his free time, he enjoys exploring new developments in Tableau.

Allison Wright is a 2021 Tableau Public featured author, a member of the 2022 Tableau's Next cohort, and a co-moderator for the Women in Dataviz Slack. She has a passion for the data community, enjoys the journey of learning, and has helped clients "see and understand data" through data visualization using Tableau. She has been working in the analytics field since 2019 and is a business intelligence developer at JLL.

This would not be possible without the #DataFam! Thank you all so much for your ongoing encouragement and support.

Table of Contents

Preface   xi

Part 1: Introduction to Tableau

1

Tableau Desktop Specialist Certification Overview   3

How will a Tableau Desktop
Specialist certification help me?   3
United States   5
United Kingdom   6

Learning Tableau Desktop basics   6
Application basics (as of April 2022)   7
Connecting to data   7

Worksheets   9
Worksheets, dashboards, and stories   10
Worksheet Data pane basics   10

Show Me charts   16
Summary   19
Knowledge check   20

2

Data Ingestion   21

Technical requirements   21
Data structure basics   22
Format   22
Basic data categorization and data types   23
Pivoted versus unpivoted data   24
Data cleanliness basics   24

Connecting to data   25
Overview of the Data Source pane   27

Formatting fields in
the Data Source pane   29
Core cleaning functions of
the Data Source pane   31

Summary   34
Knowledge check   34

3

How to Interpret Data in a Tableau Visualization   35

Technical requirements	36	Tooltips	56
Simple one-chart data visualization	36	Summary	64
Formatting a chart in Tableau	38	Knowledge check	64
Filters and actions	46		

4

Working with Dimensions, Measures, and Marks (Oh My)   65

Technical requirements	65	The Tableau Marks section	72
Grasping data dimensions	66	Tableau mark types	73
Data measures	68	Managing marks' appearance	75
Discrete versus continuous (blue versus green fields – otherwise known as pills)	69	Summary	76
		Knowledge check	76

5

Calculations and Functions Syntax   77

Technical requirements	77	Creating a (blank) calculated field	83
Tableau functions	78	Building a calculation	84
Number functions	78	Introduction to LOD expressions and parameters	86
String functions	79		
Date functions	80	LOD expressions	86
Logical functions	81	Parameters	88
Basic aggregate functions	82		
Other functions	82	Order of operations	88
		Summary	89
Creating basic calculations in Tableau	83	Knowledge check	89

Part 2: Mastering the Exam

6

Connecting to and Preparing Data   93

Technical requirements	93	Managing data properties	108
Creating live data connections and extracts	94	Unions in Tableau Desktop and join basics	112
Live versus extracted connections	94	Unions	112
Creating a live data connection	96	Join basics	117
Creating an extracted data connection and local data source	98	Summary	117
		Knowledge check	117
Creating and managing the data model	105		

7

Understanding and Creating Fundamental Charts in Tableau   119

Technical requirements	119	Scatter plot	137
Creating fundamental charts	120	Dual-axis chart	140
Bar chart	120	Filled map	143
Crosstab (text table)	122	Point maps	144
Highlight table (also known as a heat map)	127	Density maps	147
Stacked bar chart	129	Summary	149
Line chart	131	Knowledge check	149
Area chart	134		

8

Data Organization and Worksheet Analytics   151

Technical requirements	151	Working with sets	157
Organizing data	152	Applying analytics at the worksheet level	162
Grouping data	152		
Creating hierarchies	155	Managing manual/computed sorting	162

Dynamic sorting   163

Adding reference lines   **164**

Reference line instructions   164

**Working with basic
table calculations**   **167**

Basic table calculation instructions   168

**Understanding the basics
of parameters**   **171**

Creating bins and histograms   **171**

Instructions for creating a bin
and a histogram   171

Summary   **173**

Knowledge check   **174**

9

Sharing Insights   175

Technical requirements   **175**

**Formatting a visualization
for presentation**   **176**

Using colors from the Marks card   176
Configuring fonts   181
Formatting marks as shapes   188
Configuring visualization animations   190
Changing the size of marks   191
Showing and hiding legends   194

**Creating and modifying
a simple dashboard**   **196**

Dashboard pre-work   196

**Viewing and sharing
workbook data**   **218**

Sharing a workbook as a file or on a server   218
View and export underlying data   220

Summary   **220**

Knowledge check   **221**

Part 3: The Final Prep

10

Exam Preparation   225

Technical requirements   **225**

**Preparation through
examination scheduling**   **225**

Examination basics   226

Preparing for the online examination
before the day of the exam   226

Scheduling the examination and
additional preparation   227

Final examination preparation   **228**

Post-scheduling preparation   228
Exam day preparation   229
Once the examination is done   230

Summary   **230**

11

Mock Test   231

Technical requirements   231

Mock exam   231

Start the exam   232

Exam answers   240

Exam scoring   244

Basic scoring   244

Domain scoring   245

What's next?   245

Summary   246

Index   247

Other Books You May Enjoy   260

Preface

Data visualization is a common career path, or a necessary skill needed in the data analyst and data science space. A premium **business intelligence (BI)** tool used by millions is Tableau.

Globally, data visualization has taken off and changed the lives of many who are enthusiastic about it. Regardless of where you live, whether you are a new graduate or a person looking to change their career, there's space to thrive with Tableau. A Desktop Specialist verifiable certification can be your stepping stone to finding work much quicker in this space. This book is designed to give you 6 working months of knowledge needed to ace the examination within 2 weeks by focusing on specific areas of what you will be scored on while providing many practical examples you are strongly encouraged to work on and master.

By the end of this book, you will have the knowledge to not only pass the examination but also begin working in the field of data visualization. You will be able to build charts and dashboards, understand the terminology, create calculations, provide analytics, and learn formatting in Tableau. This book is also helpful for those that are required to upskill quickly for data analytics or consulting roles. Besides that, if questioned in an interview for a job requiring fundamental knowledge of Tableau, you will have the tools to confidently respond to those questions.

Who this book is for

This book is for people who are learning how to work with Tableau and require certification to establish foundational knowledge of the tool. The book assumes no knowledge of Tableau and minimal mathematical prowess. It is extensive as it is intended for those who have never opened the application to help them master all the fundamentals to pass the exam and begin to use it professionally.

What this book covers

Chapter 1, Tableau Desktop Specialist Certification Overview, is all about orienting you to the recent job market for those who possess a Tableau skillset, the Tableau tool, and some very basic applications of Tableau.

Chapter 2, Data Ingestion, begins your exploration into the data layer of Tableau. To begin creating data visualizations, you need to work with data and know how to add it to Tableau. You will learn key information about how Tableau Desktop works with data and how to perform basic preparation in the tool.

Chapter 3, How to Interpret Data in a Tableau Visualization, provides an introduction to working with a Tableau sheet after ingesting data. It also teaches you how to create a basic chart and about formatting in a based-in-real life iteration process for a team.

Chapter 4, Working with Dimensions, Measures, and Marks (Oh My), going beyond the basics covered in *Chapters 1* and *3*, this chapter goes into detail with examples of applying data dimensions, data measures, and discrete versus continuous fields, and provides an introduction to the Tableau Marks section.

Chapter 5, Calculations and Functions Syntax, covers calculations and functions syntax. The examination does not go very deep into this topic, but expects a working knowledge of the types of calculations and functions and how to work with them. This chapter is more technical than the previous one but focuses on the essential and commonly applied functions and calculation basics.

Chapter 6, Connecting to and Preparing Data, extending the basic knowledge of working with data from *Chapter 2*, provides more technical applications of data elements, including working with the Tableau Data Model, managing data properties, and working with live data versus extracts.

Chapter 7, Understanding and Creating Fundamental Charts in Tableau, teaches you about 11 common Tableau charts covered in the examination, with step-by-step instructions to build each one, while providing details of when to use them and insights that can be explored. It's a very hands-on chapter and will help you feel like a Tableau developer.

Chapter 8, Data Organization and Worksheet Analytics, going beyond creating charts, illustrates the additional analytics and data organization a developer would apply to a worksheet to provide additional functionality and insights. The organization portion of the chapter includes the hands-on management of sets, groups, bins, and hierarchies; the analytics portion includes creating a histogram, applying reference lines, and the basics of table calculations, with an introduction to parameters.

Chapter 9, Sharing Insights, concluding the instructional section of the book, is a substantial chapter that dives into the real magic of Tableau. It details additional and more advanced, but necessary, formatting options, creating a basic dashboard and the additional actions and functionality dashboards provide, and finally, how a dashboard or its data can be shared with others.

Chapter 10, Exam Preparation, as many people are not experienced with taking proctored examinations, covers what to expect from the exam and how to make sure you are ready to take the examination, and is filled with tips to make sure you are successful.

Chapter 11, Mock Test, now that you have learned the fundamentals of Tableau and taking a proctored examination, puts those skills to the test with a mock exam. It follows a similar weighting and methodology to the actual Tableau Desktop Specialist certification.

To get the most out of this book

This book is aimed at those who are new to Tableau or have never opened the application. It assumes no knowledge of Tableau. Although all exercises come with step-by-step instructions and prior knowledge is not required, having a background in Excel formulas, SQL, and/or using data visualizations in another tool will reduce the learning curve and help you pick things up quicker. You will need to set aside 25-40 hours over 2 weeks to read, practice, take the mock exam, and review the additional study materials.

Software/hardware covered in the book	Operating system requirements
Tableau Desktop (2022.1)	Windows and macOS
Tableau Public (optional)	Windows and macOS

Throughout the book, you will be working with examples utilizing Tableau Desktop. To get the most from the book, please download the Tableau Desktop application, which offers a free trial for 2 weeks every time a new version is released. However, downloading the free Tableau Public application will give you most of the features and a playground to publish exercises for absolutely no cost.

Conventions used

There are a number of text conventions used throughout this book.

`Code in text`: Indicates code words in text, database table names, folder names, filenames, file extensions, pathnames, dummy URLs, user input, and Twitter handles. Here is an example: "Mount the downloaded `WebStorm-10*.dmg` disk image file as another disk in your system."

Bold: Indicates a new term, an important word, or words that you see onscreen. For instance, words in menus or dialog boxes appear in **bold**. Here is an example: "Select **System info** from the **Administration** panel."

> **Tips or important notes**
> Appear like this.

Get in touch

Feedback from our readers is always welcome.

General feedback: If you have questions about any aspect of this book, email us at `customercare@packtpub.com` and mention the book title in the subject of your message.

Errata: Although we have taken every care to ensure the accuracy of our content, mistakes do happen. If you have found a mistake in this book, we would be grateful if you would report this to us. Please visit `www.packtpub.com/support/errata` and fill in the form.

Piracy: If you come across any illegal copies of our works in any form on the internet, we would be grateful if you would provide us with the location address or website name. Please contact us at `copyright@packtpub.com` with a link to the material.

If you are interested in becoming an author: If there is a topic that you have expertise in and you are interested in either writing or contributing to a book, please visit `authors.packtpub.com`.

Share Your Thoughts

Once you've read *Tableau Desktop Specialist Certification*, we'd love to hear your thoughts! Scan the QR code below to go straight to the Amazon review page for this book and share your feedback.

`https://packt.link/r/1-801-81013-3`

Your review is important to us and the tech community and will help us make sure we're delivering excellent quality content.

Download a free PDF copy of this book

Thanks for purchasing this book!

Do you like to read on the go but are unable to carry your print books everywhere?

Is your eBook purchase not compatible with the device of your choice?

Don't worry, now with every Packt book you get a DRM-free PDF version of that book at no cost.

Read anywhere, any place, on any device. Search, copy, and paste code from your favorite technical books directly into your application.

The perks don't stop there, you can get exclusive access to discounts, newsletters, and great free content in your inbox daily

Follow these simple steps to get the benefits:

1. Scan the QR code or visit the link below

https://packt.link/free-ebook/9781801810135

2. Submit your proof of purchase
3. That's it! We'll send your free PDF and other benefits to your email directly

Part 1: Introduction to Tableau

A Tableau developer requires basic knowledge of Tableau desktop and data ingestion to begin to master the fundamentals of the tool and start to absorb the knowledge required for the Tableau Desktop Specialist Examination.

The first part includes five chapters, which will cover an introduction to the examination; related work; how to ingest data and work with the data pane in Tableau; how to begin to understand the data with iterative hands-on work; dimensions, measures, and marks; and, finally, digging deeper into the basics of Tableau functions and calculation.

By the end of this part, you will have learned about the examination and how to begin working with the tool, understood the basics of functions and calculation, worked iteratively in Tableau, and understood some of the elementary formatting work that can be done. This section will set you up to dig deeper in the next section to really begin to master Tableau's fundamentals to help you with the examination, as well as provide some direct applications.

This part comprises the following chapters:

- *Chapter 1, Tableau Desktop Specialist Certification Overview*
- *Chapter 2, Data Ingestion*
- *Chapter 3, How to Interpret the Data in a Data Visualization*
- *Chapter 4, Working with Dimensions, Measures, and Marks*
- *Chapter 5, Calculations and Functions Syntax*

1

Tableau Desktop Specialist Certification Overview

Tableau is a premium data visualization tool used for BI that has an impact on a wide variety of stakeholders. This chapter focuses on the Tableau Desktop Specialist certification's purpose, relevant careers, and the tool with a basic look at default charting. Understanding these fundamentals will provide you with the necessary background before your certification journey begins.

In this chapter, we will cover the following topics:

- How will a Tableau Desktop certification help me?
- Top careers and their relationship to learning Tableau
- Tableau Desktop basics
- Tableau basic Show Me charts

Let's begin by covering what a Tableau Desktop Specialist certification is and what it can mean to you.

How will a Tableau Desktop Specialist certification help me?

Many people learn Tableau and never receive a certification. Although they have the skills to pass the certification, many people are passed over by recruiters and employers, who will look for people who passed the certification first. In this section, you will learn how the certification will help you and the relevant careers you can explore through the certification. Many careers include data visualization as a primary or secondary focus. Tableau is considered one of the most popular and widely used data visualization tools. Many employers require verifiable evidence that their prospective employees can use the tool and contribute. Unlike other official Tableau certifications, the Tableau Desktop Specialist certification is permanent and is easily verifiable by sharing a link to the online verification. It can also be verified from LinkedIn and other social sites. It's important to have a verifiable certification from the software company that's easy to confirm so that potential technical recruiters and employers seeking talent can immediately confirm your qualifications and reach out to you without leaving the site.

It breaks down your capabilities not only with the tool but also your general abilities to analyze data and data presentation, which is also helpful to support your general functionality as a person who is data-capable.

Last year, I took the test as it just changed from a *hands-on* to a *knowledge-based* format. This book will focus on the new format, which has new and more complex challenges compared to the prior version.

Here is the certification I earned last year:

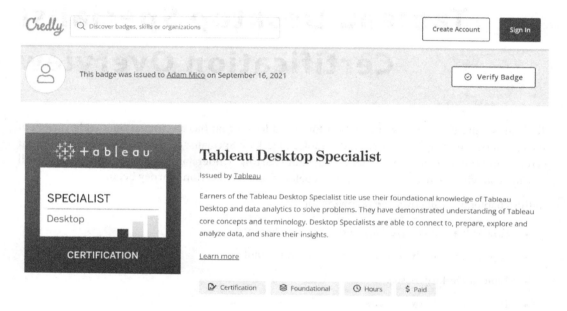

Figure 1.1 – Adam Mico's Tableau Desktop Specialist verification page

There are many jobs where this certification has significant usefulness, several of which are included in glassdoor.com's 50 Best Jobs in America and 25 Best Jobs in the UK for 2022. The following is a breakdown of the rankings:

Rank| Job Title | Median Base Salary (US $ | UK £) | Job Satisfaction | Job Openings | Job Requirement Likelihood (Low-Possible-Primary-Principal).

To help streamline and provide a consistent understanding between the US and UK glassdoor.com job rankings, this defined breakdown will be used for both the US and UK sections that follow.

United States

United States glassdoor.com job rankings that can require or provide a benefit with a Tableau Desktop Specialist certification are as follows:

- #3 | Data Scientist | $120,000 | 4.1/5 | 10,071 | Possible Requirement (and growing)

  The data scientist job is constantly evolving. That evolution is to help create discovered insights that are more approachable for business stakeholders. Those stakeholders need clearer insights in a language they understand. One significant approach is data visualization. This comes into more focus with companies that do not have a dedicated data visualization team.

- #7 | Data Engineer | $113,960 | 4.0/5 | 11,821 | Possible Requirement (and growing)

  The primary role of many data engineers is not to create data visualizations (especially in larger organizations), but it is often a necessity to create and learn to develop data visualizations to vet the data, provide a proof of concept, or possibly develop visualizations if the company does not have a dedicated data visualization team.

- #8 | Software Engineer | $116,638 | 3.9/5 | 64,155 | Principal Requirement (Tableau)

  A Tableau Software Engineer or Software Developer's primary role is to develop data visualizations, though there are other tasks, such as working with business teams, technical teams, and stakeholders. As a current Principal Software Engineer, I can share that having at least a Tableau Desktop Specialist certification was essential for even the basic consideration of my role.

- #20 | Consultant | $90,748 | 3.9/5 | 17,728 | Principal Requirement (Data Consultant)

  Similar to a Tableau Software Engineer, many consultancies have data consultants. Their responsibilities cover the data gamut from data engineering/modeling/preparation to a deliverable top-class data visualization. I recently worked as a Tableau Evangelist for a data-focused consultancy. Certifications are essential to that role as special Tableau certifications are needed to help partners retain services with Tableau. Having a certification pre-hire helps establish that you can attain those certifications.

- #35 | Data Analyst | $74,224 | 4.0/5 | 13,657 | Primary Requirement

  From 2017 to 2021, I worked as a data analyst and business automation specialist and as a senior analyst for the final 2 years of my employment. That role was new and only became possible for me because of the internal development I did with Tableau. For the entirety, at least 20% of my job was related to Tableau. In the current data analyst skill stack, data visualization is a necessity.

- #36 | Business Analyst | $81,556 | 3.9/5 | 15,238 | Primary-Principal Requirement

  In many cases, companies may employ data analysts and business analysts interchangeably, depending on their structure. Although there is some specialization with larger companies, which may restrict some of the data visualization needs of a data analyst, with business analysts, that's even less likely. Where a data analyst may need to work more on the backend, much of a business analyst's work is more frontend- and stakeholder-focused.

United Kingdom

The United Kingdom's glassdoor.com job rankings that can require or provide a benefit with a Tableau Desktop Specialist certification are as follows:

- #5 | Data Scientist | £49,449| 4.2/5 | 1,011 | Possible (and growing)

    For the description, please see #3 for the US.

- #9 | Front End Engineer | £43,803 | 4.2/5 | 1,529 | Principal Requirement (Tableau)

    In this specialty, the employee's experience is related to that of a business analyst but is someone who works more closely in Agile (likely) project teams, which would likely include backend developers/engineers and subject matter experts.

- #11 | Software Engineer | £50,060 | 3.9/5 | 3,599 | Principal Requirement (Tableau)

    For the description, please see #8 for the US.

- #24 | Consultant | £46,215 | 3.9/5 |1,498 | Principal Requirement (Data Consultant)

    For the description, please see #20 for the US.

Entry to very lucrative, growing, and impactful careers are possible with a Tableau Desktop Specialist certification. Furthermore, there are many more roles that are transitioning to a generalist approach as businesses are looking for potential ways to better understand their data and be proactive rather than reactive. In recent years, in my professional experience, people are leaving the once-a-week/month/quarter email delivery of static infographics to interact with data visualizations displaying live or more recent data for more effective questions, analysis, and iterations. You may be checking this book out as you have a new job requirement to learn Tableau and validate those learnings with a certification.

Now that you understand the importance and impact a certification can have, we need to explore the fundamentals of the tool itself.

Learning Tableau Desktop basics

You must learn the basics of Tableau before exploring the application. To complete the Tableau Desktop Specialist certification, fundamental knowledge of the correct terminology will provide a strong basis for further development. In future chapters, we will deep dive into each relevant component of the application in more detail.

Application basics (as of April 2022)

Here are the elementary items that will help you understand Tableau's accessibility, pricing, release cadence, and what data it can support:

- A desktop application with a separate application for Windows and Mac.
- The desktop application includes a 2-week free trial but is $70 per month thereafter.

> **Pro tip**
> Download the Tableau Public application at `https://public.tableau.com/app/discover`. It will have all the features you will need to understand the concepts for the Tableau Desktop certification and is free.

- The user interface and supporting documentation are available in the following languages: English, French, German, Italian, Spanish, Brazilian Portuguese, Japanese, Korean, Traditional Chinese, and Simplified Chinese.
- The release cadence is quarterly but is backward compatible.
- Supports many data sources.
- Capable of handling millions of rows of data.
- Can support code and scripts, but is mostly utilized with drag-and-drop functionality with the ability to create maps, field hierarchies, dimensional groups and sets, calculations (from simple to very complex), and parameters. It can also utilize extensions that are not part of the out-of-the-box functionality.

To begin developing data visualizations, you need data. The next section will cover the basics of connecting to data.

Connecting to data

To use Tableau, a user needs to connect to data. The number of data sources you can connect to is ever-growing, with a multitude of connectors developed by companies in association with Tableau to ensure scalable connectivity. Here is a screenshot of the data connection page:

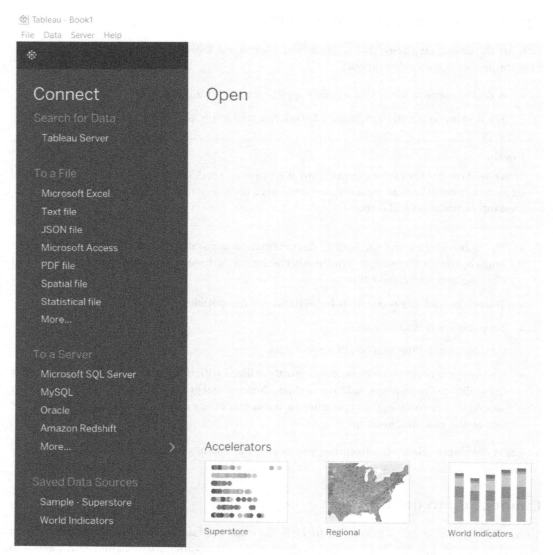

Figure 1.2 – Connect to Data from Tableau 2021.4

With Tableau, you can connect from the following services:

- **Tableau Server** (or Tableau Online): Tableau Server data sources are data sources published in the Tableau environment. They can be sourced from any supported file and server but hosted and formatted for usage in Tableau Server.

- **A file**: Tableau supports a significant section of files that may potentially be used, from CSV (referred to as a part of a *text file*) to PDFs to statistical and spatial files.

- **A non-Tableau Server**: So long as a user has credentials, many servers have dedicated connectors. Even if your server is not inherently supported through dedicated connectors, there are ad hoc JDBC and ODBC database connectivity options.

Unlike many other data visualization tools, Tableau supports an extensive and ever-growing list of data sources. In every release, it's very likely to see even more supported and named connection options.

Worksheets

Worksheets are the next order of the application. Once connected to a data source, Tableau highlights **Sheet 1** (default name) so that you can explore the data further. The following screenshot shows an example of this:

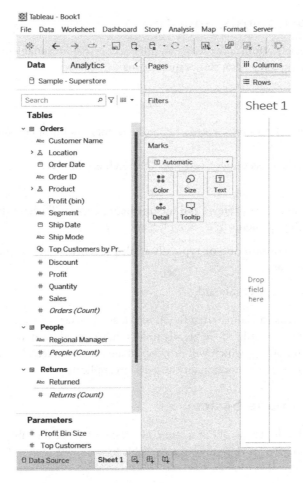

Figure 1.3 – Worksheet using Tableau's default Sample – Superstore data

After connecting to a data source, the application will direct you to a sheet, as shown in the preceding screenshot. On the left, there will be a **Data** pane. This hosts your dimensional fields and measurement fields. To work with those fields, you can drag and drop them onto one of the following areas shown on the right-hand side of *Figure 1.3*:

- **Columns**: Stacks data dimensions from left to right in a visualization
- **Rows**: Displays data dimensions vertically in a visualization
- **Marks**: A section that adds context, dimensions, and context to the visualization

You have learned how to connect to data and the basics of its structure. I will begin sharing more about the visualization application in the next section.

Worksheets, dashboards, and stories

At the bottom of the application, some icons identify access to additional worksheets, dashboards, and stories. The following screenshot shows those icons:

Figure 1.4 – Worksheet, dashboard, and story icons (respectively)

Let's learn more about the preceding screenshot. Tableau has a hierarchical structure for dashboard building, as follows:

- Worksheets are at the lowest level and the one item people will spend the most time using to create visualization elements (charts, tables, and so on)
- Dashboards can contain one or typically multiple worksheets so that you can create an interactive visualization
- Stories hold at least one dashboard

Selecting any of these icons will launch that function. Most end users will see a dashboard when they use the tool as stories are not utilized frequently unless they're used for demonstration purposes (as there are more modern options, which will be covered later). Worksheets can be displayed on their own, but dashboards have more functionality and design applications.

Worksheet Data pane basics

The **Data** pane is the developer's working section. Here, they can see the tables and fields associated with the data source and get a preview of what is available to work with. *Figure 1.5* provides an example of how that looks:

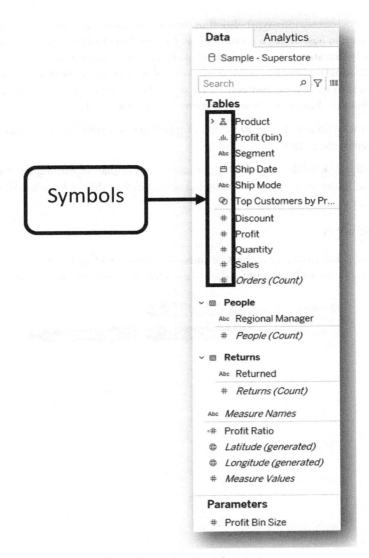

Figure 1.5 – Worksheet data pane

A lot is going on in *Figure 1.5*. The following list details some of the basics associated with it:

- Tableau displays a faint line between dimensions (or qualitative data) and measures (or quantitative data). This faint line is a visual indicator to help users determine what can be used as a dimension and what can be used as a measure as each has a very different purpose for data visualization. This can be seen in the **People** table between the **Regional Manager** and **People (Count)** fields.

- Tableau provides various symbols left of the field by table name to show whether it's a string (**abc**, as seen in **Segment**), a number (#, as seen in **Discount**), geography (a globe, as seen in **Latitude (generated)**), a date (calendar, as seen in **Ship Date**), a hierarchy (hierarchy icon, as seen in **Product**), a bin (bar graph or bin symbol, as seen in **Profit (bin)**), or sets (overlapping circles, as seen in **Top Customers…**). These symbols are there to help users quickly scan data to see what they have to work with and how it can be utilized.

- Any field with an equals sign to the left of it (as seen in **Profit Ratio**) means it's a calculation that's been made in Tableau.

- Beneath the table fields, the available parameters are displayed. Although parameters can only be created in the same way as a calculated field can, they do not have equals signs in front of them like calculated fields.

Columns and rows

Beyond the **Data** pane, you can explore **Columns** and **Rows**. Adding measures to rows or columns creates a quantitative axis where a dimension to a row or column generates a header:

Figure 1.6 – Columns and Rows (Sample – Superstore)

With just a few drags and drops, you can create a useful chart. For example, as shown in the preceding screenshot, we can drag and drop **Order Date** to **Columns** (which displays as a discrete date – that is, **Year**), and then **Segment** (dimensional string) and **Sales** (a measure that defaults to **Sum**, resulting in a sum of sales) to **Rows**.

Marks

The **Marks** card is used to make updates to the default visualization. It is responsible for showing additional dimensionality and adding color and labels. It can be utilized to update charts, add colors, mark labels, add reference paths, shapes, use window calculations, enhance tooltips, and for sizing (all of which will be covered later), and additional options. The following is a visual representation of the **Marks** card:

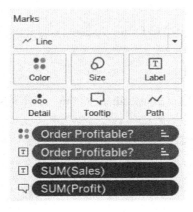

Figure 1.7 – Marks card

In *Figure 1.8*, I have the same structure in **Columns** and **Rows** as in *Figure 1.6* but modified the chart using the adjustments I made in *Figure 1.7* in the **Marks** section:

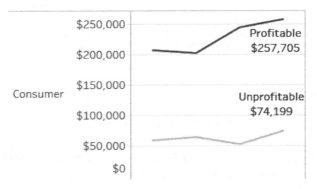

Figure 1.8 – Updated visual

In the chart in *Figure 1.8*, I wanted to see what sales came from profitable versus unprofitable orders. I colored by whether an item was profitable (top mark with the four dots). This coloring created a separate dimension for whether the order was profitable. In *Figure 1.8*, I can see that most of my sales came from **Profitable** orders in the **Consumer** segment. In the text of the line charts (*Figure 1.8*), I wanted to show which line represented what was profitable and the most recent sales (or what the sales for each were in 2021).

> **Note**
> Calculations will be demonstrated in future chapters, beginning with *Chapter 5*.

Filters

The following screenshot shows how a basic filter can impact what is displayed to a user:

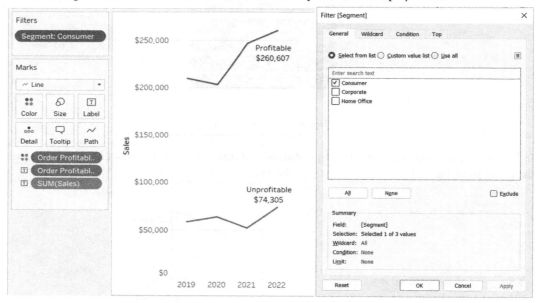

Figure 1.9 – Filter on Segment

Filters provide a developer or end user more flexibility to see what they need to see and ignore the rest. The preceding visualization only includes the **Consumer** segment. However, it is simple to show and/or hide a filter to determine whether you want end users to access the filters on a dashboard.

Quick measure adjustments

Tableau provides quick updates to measures. It's vital to be able to display your data in the way that's intended. *Figure 1.10* shows an example of this with additional information:

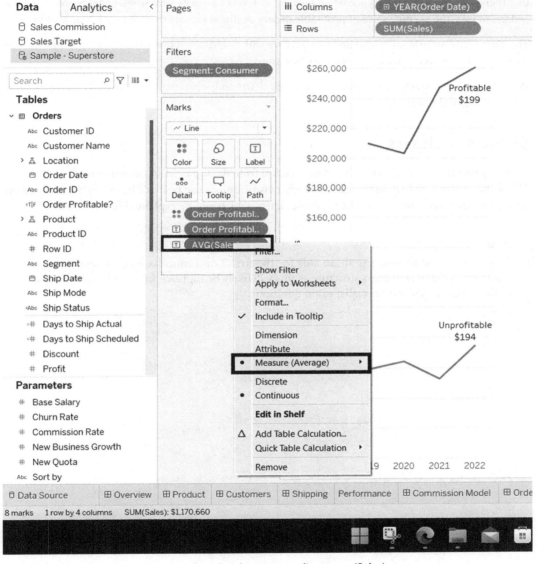

Figure 1.10 – Quick measure adjustment (Sales)

With a couple of clicks, a user can quickly adjust the chart's measurements and the text of those measurements by adjusting the measure. In this instance, the end user did not want to see the total sales of what was profitable, but rather the average sales of orders profitable versus not profitable to determine any trends or whether they should consider a cut-off point. What they saw immediately is that there was very little difference when looking at average sales by year when considering profitable orders; in fact, the average sales of profitable orders declined rapidly over the past couple of years.

There are many more features and items to uncover with Tableau, but this gives you a brief introduction to some of the power of its very basic core functions.

With that, we have previewed a couple of the quick charts and adjustments we can make using columns, rows, marks, and filters.

Show Me charts

Tableau provides a list of charts that can be accessed from the top right-hand corner of the application. This feature intends to help users determine what visualizations can be made based on the data utilized. The following screenshot shows the available charts, which will be explained further shortly:

> **Note**
>
> Most users tend to only use these aids for the first 2 or 3 months, but it's very helpful to understand the data to chart structure as this will likely be captured in some fashion in several of the Tableau Desktop Specialist exam questions.

For **lines** (discrete) try

1 date 📅

0 or more Dimensions

1 or more Measures

Figure 1.11 – Tableau's Show Me charts

Tableau provides a list of 24 charts that are of great help to those new to using Tableau. The data on the worksheet highlights the usable charts and grays out or lightly shades out the ones where you do not have enough data needed for these charts. Even if you do not have the data you need to apply to the sheet, you can hover over the chart type to reveal the number of dimensions or fields of qualitative data and measures of quantitative data. Even more, it points out special fields such as date fields (as referenced in the lower portion of *Figure 1.11*).

You don't need to know all of these charts by heart and you may not necessarily use some of these charts frequently, but it helps to learn the basics of these to better understand how to utilize the tool.

Here, we will cover the charts shown in *Figure 1.11* from left to right while moving down, repeating this for each of the eight rows of charts. For example, chart 1 represents the chart shown at the top left, while chart 24 represents the chart shown at the bottom right. The format will be as follows:

Chart Name | Brief Explanation | Basic Data Needed

Let's take a look:

1. Text Table | A data breakdown similar to a spreadsheet | 1+ dimension and 1+ measure
2. Heat Map | Similar to a text table, but uses shapes and colors to identify data | 1+ dimension, and 1 or 2 measures
3. Highlight Table | A data breakdown similar to a spreadsheet, but with conditional formatting | 1+ dimension and 1+ measure
4. Symbol Map | A map that commonly uses sized/colored filled circles to provide contextual insight | 1 Geographic data dimension, 0+ other dimensions, and 0 to 2 measures
5. Filled Map | A map that uses filled geography rather than sized marks to provide contextual insight | 1 Geographic data dimension, 0+ other dimensions, and 0 to 1 measures
6. Pie Chart | A sliced circle based on the size relative to the whole circle (or pie) | 1 or more dimensions and 1 or 2 measures
7. Horizontal Bar Chart | A dimensional horizontal-stacked set of bars sized by value | 0+ dimensions and 1+ measures
8. Stacked Bar Chart | A dimensionally stacked set of bars sized by value, broken down by multiple dimensions in a bar | 1+ dimensions and 1+ measures
9. Side-By-Side Bar Chart | A dimensionally unstacked set of bars (rather side by side) sized by value, broken down by multiple dimensions in a bar | 1+ dimensions and 1+ measures (3+ fields required in total)
10. Tree Map | Similar to a pie chart, but each "slice" is stacked in descending order of volume (usually) and sized from top left to bottom right to demonstrate a hierarchy in nested triangles of a different size | 1+ dimensions and 1 to 2 measures
11. Circle View Chart | Uses a circle to provide comparative analysis for many dimensions | 1+ dimensions and 1+ measures

12. Side-By-Side Circle View Chart | Like a circle view chart, but provides additional analysis of additional dimensions side by side | 3+ fields required, 1+ dimensions, and 1+ measures

13. Continuous Line Chart | Used to track a measure over time with clean lines from the start to end date | A date field (continuous), 0+ dimensions, and 1+ measures

14. Discrete Line Chart | Similar to a continuous line chart, but the dates are discrete, which breaks up lines by dimensions | A date field (discrete), 0+ dimensions, and 1+ measures

15. Dual Line Chart | Combines multiple axes of multiple measures to create two single line charts | A date field (discrete), 0+ dimensions, and 2 measures

16. Continuous Area Chart | Used to track a measure over time with clean lines from the start to the end date (effectively a filled continuous line chart) | A date field (continuous), 0+ dimensions, and 1+ measures

17. Discrete Area Chart | Similar to a continuous area chart, but the dates are discrete, which breaks up lines by dimensions (effectively a filled discrete line chart) | 1 date field (discrete), 0+ dimensions, and 1+ measures

18. Dual Combination Chart | Similar to a dual line chart, but one of the lines is substituted for a bar chart to get a bar versus line chart effect | A date field (discrete), 0+ dimensions, and 2 measures

19. Scatter Plot Chart | Utilizes measures to create a comparison of numerical data over the X and Y axes | 0+ dimensions and 2 to 4 measures

20. Histogram Chart | Creates a bin of a measure to look at the data distribution | 1 measure (creates a bin in the **Data** pane, but not available for all measures)

21. Box and Whisker Plot Chart | Shows data in its quartile distribution with individual data points | Requires at least one dimension or disaggregate, 0+ dimensions, and 1+ measures

22. Gantt Chart | Used most frequently to display project timelines | 1 date field, 1+ dimensions, and 2 measures

23. Bullet Graph Chart | Used as a bar chart, but with additional context – think comparing an actual with a target | 0+ dimensions and 2 measures

24. Packed Bubbles Chart | Used similarly to a tree map, but packs filled circles together by size (and often color) to fit randomly into a user-defined container | 1+ dimensions and 1 to 2 measures

Summary

In this chapter, we covered what purpose the Tableau Desktop Specialist certification has for your career and looked at some highly sought-after careers that the certification can apply to. Then, we covered the basics of Tableau, which included looking at the application, providing an introduction to data ingestion, providing an introduction to tool basics, and looking at in-tool charting resources.

In the next chapter, we will dive deeper into data ingestion as it applies to using Tableau.

Knowledge check

To check your knowledge of this chapter, here are three questions that this chapter's material will help you answer. The questions that have been selected aren't intended to trick you, but provide you with a learning benchmark to give you a foundational understanding to help prepare you for the exam. The answers are marked in italics:

1. What is the cost of the Tableau Public application?

    A. $70 per month, billed annually

    B. $150 per year

    C. Part of the Tableau Desktop license, so no cost on its own, but the same cost as Tableau Desktop

    D. *Free*

2. In *Figure 1.6*, in what years are consumer sales less than $300,000?

    A. *2018 and 2019*

    B. 2019 and 2020

    C. 2020 and 2021

    D. 2018 only

3. What type of data is contained in dimensions?

    A. Quantitative data

    B. *Qualitative data*

    C. No data

    D. None of the above

2
Data Ingestion

Data is the essential building block for **data visualization**. It is no different in Tableau. To create visualizations in Tableau, data is required. Data can be as small as one column or field and one row or hundreds of fields and many millions of rows.

One of Tableau's greatest strengths is its ability to work with robust and diverse sets of data. Before using Tableau, you need to determine what will work with your use case of applying data to Tableau Desktop.

In this chapter, you will learn about some of the core concepts required for the Tableau Desktop certification. Connecting to and preparing data comprises 25% of the exam. It is also an essential building block for what will be covered in the following chapters.

In this chapter, we will cover the following topics:

- Data structure basics
- Connecting to data
- Overview of the Data Source pane
- Formatting fields in the Data Source pane

Technical requirements

You will need one of the following to apply the hands-on learning from this chapter:

- A Tableau Desktop application. Most versions will work with the exam, but for the best results, use version 2021.1 or later. It can be downloaded from https://www.tableau.com/products/desktop/download. This version is not free but does provide a 2-week trial. If you are a student attending an accredited university, you can receive a desktop license for free for 1 year. Trials cannot be extended if they've been used previously, but you will be able to get a free 2-week trial with every quarterly upgrade of the desktop version.

- A version that meets all of the functionality needs of Tableau Desktop but is free is Tableau Public. It doesn't have all the data and extension functionality of the Tableau Desktop application, but everything you need for the Tableau Desktop certification. It is available here: `https://public.tableau.com/en-us/s/download`. If you've downloaded it already, please use version 2021.1 or later.

You will also require the Superstore Sales dataset to work with this chapter. It comes with the Tableau Desktop application automatically, but it can also be pulled into the Tableau Public application if you download it from the Tableau resources at `https://public.tableau.com/en-us/s/resources?qt-overview_resources=1#qt-overview_resources`.

Data structure basics

In this section, you will understand what the entry points for data ingestion into Tableau are. There are many data components,, and each data component needs to be understood to grasp the context. You will learn about Tableau's data structure and how it is prepared for data visualization. You will require this knowledge to understand related questions in the exam.

Format

Data needs to be in a spreadsheet-like structure. That structure can come from a variety of sources, including a CSV/text file, a server (for example, Amazon Redshift, Microsoft SQL Server, or Tableau), and many more.

To get the best out of the data source, make sure all the rows and columns are accounted for. There should be no blank rows on top so that Tableau does not create false headings or blank rows on the left of the table, which will create false fields – however, those false fields can be cleaned up with Data Interpreter in Tableau. Since many people will be using Excel or a similar spreadsheet tool, the following screenshot (*Figure 2.1*) is based on Excel/CSV to introduce data sourcing in Tableau:

	A	B	C	D	E	F	G
1	Category	Order Date	Segment	Sales Target			
2	Office Supplies	1/3/2018	Consumer	15			
3	Office Supplies	1/4/2018	Home Office	300			
4	Office Supplies	1/5/2018	Consumer	21			
5	Furniture	1/6/2018	Home Office	2316			
6	Office Supplies	1/6/2018	Consumer	17			
7	Office Supplies	1/6/2018	Corporate	14			
8	Office Supplies	1/6/2018	Home Office	699			
9	Technology	1/6/2018	Home Office	1068			

Row 1 and Columns A-D: Data Columns or Fields

Row 2-9 from Columns A-D: Rows of Data

Figure 2.1 – Excel data source example (from Sales Target (US), Tableau)

Here, we took a small table from the Superstore Sales data called `Sales Target (US)`. It is an Excel table that we will use throughout this section to explain some of Tableau's data features.

Data columns/fields

The top rows of any data source in Tableau will be used as the default fields for analysis. These fields are what you will see when working with the desktop application. These will contain the named dimensions or measures utilized for a visualization. This can be seen in *Figure 2.1* as the bold text in row 1 (columns A-D). The field names from this data source are **Category**, **Order Date**, **Segment**, and **Sales Target**. Tableau is smart enough to recognize a table and exclude the data outside of the table, even in the same sheet, if provided, and will not pull additional data outside the table.

Rows of data or data granularity

Each row after row 1 contains the actual data represented in the headers and will illustrate the visualization. The number of fields represents the data's aggregation level. In *Figure 2.1*, we can see that the data is captured by **Category**, **Order Date**, and **Segment**, with **Sales Target** as the measure for those fields. For example, row 5 shows **Furniture** under **Category**, with an **Order Date** of **1/6/2018**. Its **Segment** is **Home Office**, and its **Sales Target** is **2316**. Tableau can manipulate the data along these lines but cannot disaggregate further unless it is manipulated by adding additional data.

> **Tips**
>
> If you're working with a CSV file, convert it into an explicit table in your spreadsheet tool to make sure you are working with the intended structure.
>
> If you're working with multiple data sources, make sure that you have a field that you can use as a key field to link other tables.

Basic data categorization and data types

Tableau can make a good-quality guess about the type of the data that comes in, especially if it is structured well. For example, using *Figure 2.1*, Tableau will be able to recognize that **Category** and **Segment** are string fields, **Order Date** is a date field, and **Sales Target** is a numerical measure. Later in this chapter, you will be introduced to the basics of category manipulation, but for most well-structured data fields, this is something Tableau does well.

Go to `https://help.tableau.com/current/pro/desktop/en-us/datafields_typesandroles_datatypes.htm` for more information on Tableau Desktop icons and related data types.

> **Note**
>
> The tool is designed to create hierarchies, sets, groups, bins, and calculations using the fields that come into the application.

Pivoted versus unpivoted data

Tableau generally works better with more rows than more columns. For example, sometimes, you may get data coming in with a date being a new field. For example, data may come in without a `Sales Target` field and each date contains a numeric value in its rows, which represents the sales target for that date. That data is considered wide and unpivoted.

Pivoted data is tall with more rows, but fewer fields. Not only can Tableau understand it better, but you also have more flexibility with charting, calculations, and so forth. Unlike other programs, it is designed to work with many rows of data without performance issues. In *Figure 2.2*, even in the small sample of data provided, you can see the significant difference based on dates acting as separate fields rather than a singular date field and where the translation pitfalls may lie:

	A	B	C	D	E	F	G	H	I
1	Category	Segment	1/3/2018	1/4/2018	1/5/2018	1/6/2018	Row 1 and Columns A-F: Data Columns or Fields		
2	Office Supplies	Consumer	15		21	17			
3	Office Supplies	Home Office		300		699	Row 2-6 from Columns A-F: Rows of Data		
4	Office Supplies	Corporate				14			
5	Furniture	Home Office				2316			
6	Technology	Home Office				1068			

Figure 2.2 – Wider data version of the Excel data source example (from Sales Target (US), Tableau)

Figure 2.2 now has six fields of data and five rows. The **Order Date** and **Sales Target** fields are absent. Individual date fields show associated sales targets. Besides seeing null values, each date field is no longer a date but a heading for a numerical field. Besides knowing it is a number, there is no way of knowing what that number represents (unless there is a separate (and new) field named **Measure** and **Sales Target** for each row). Imagine how complex it would be to work with this data if it had more dates, segments, and categories.

> **Tip**
> If the data includes dates, make sure the data includes a date field rather than an individual field for each date.

Data cleanliness basics

A visualization is only as good as its data quality. I have long considered the data visualization aspect at the very tip of the data visualization iceberg:

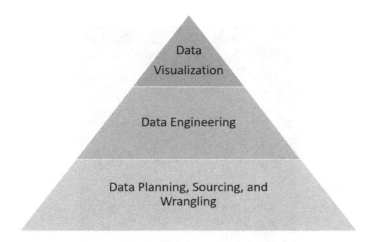

Figure 2.3 – The basic data visualization iceberg (or pyramid)

Many pieces need to come together to visualize data. Some of these aspects were referenced earlier, but cleanliness and consistency for performance, accuracy, and scalability are just as important.

Since Tableau defines fields based on the data included in the rows, each field must represent its intended category. Tableau forgives null values, but if, for example, *Figure 2.2* had **No** instead of a null value for **Furniture** on **1/3/18**, that small change would change the **1/3/18** field from a numerical category to a text string (or categorical value).

> **Important**
>
> Before visualizing, it is imperative to vet the data to verify that it is functioning as it should. A simple and basic way to do this is to see what fields are not acting as intended and see why – often, this is due to an unintended data type in the field.

Connecting to data

As mentioned in *Chapter 1, Tableau Desktop Specialist Certification Overview*, you can connect to the data via a server (Tableau or another) or a file and can also connect to one or multiple data sources. On Tableau Desktop, you should try to connect with the same type of data source to get the highest performance. For example, if you're using Microsoft Excel, other Excel files will work more effectively.

For the basic connection, I will connect to **Sample – Superstore** (see *Figure 2.4*), which is the default sample dataset from Tableau. It is what many tutorials and help guides from Tableau and the community are based on:

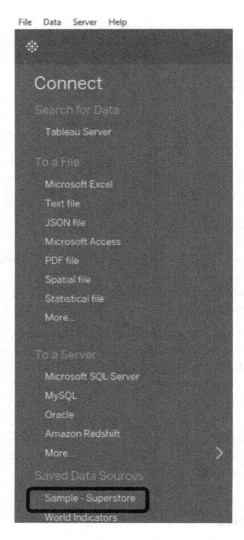

Figure 2.4 – Sample – Superstore default saved data source from Tableau Desktop

Simply select **Sample – Superstore**. Once connected, you will be taken to **Sheet 1**, where you can see all the tables and fields it contains (unless other data sources were added to the data pane before this data source was brought in):

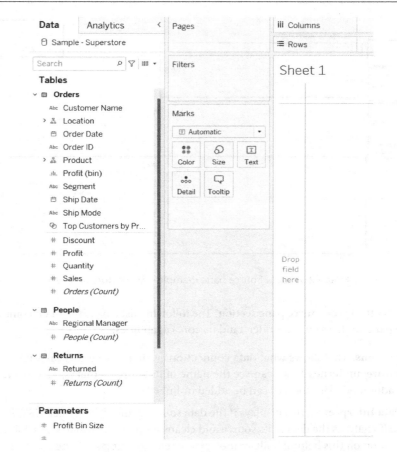

Figure 2.5 – Tableau accesses the sheet showing the tables and
fields from the data source selected in Figure 2.1

We talked about the very basics of what was displayed on **Sheet 1** in *Chapter 1*, *Tableau Desktop Specialist Certification Overview*, but now, we need to go to the **Data Source** pane at the bottom left of *Figure 2.5*.

Overview of the Data Source pane

The **Data Source** pane is the introductory block for building any Tableau visualization. From here, you can see how the data is ingested and how basic data types are cleaned, and see how the data is connected before working with it in Tableau. Knowing about the **Data Source** pane is not only relevant for the exam, but it also makes data visualization more intuitive:

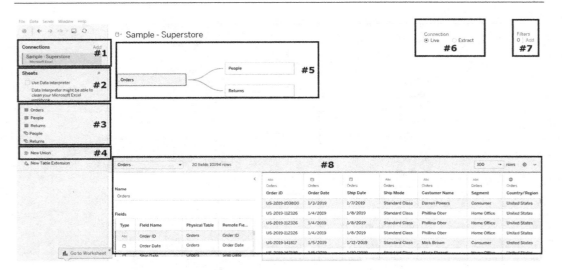

Figure 2.6 – Data Source pane (Sample – Superstore dataset)

Figure 2.6 shows the **Data Source** pane section. The following list covers the main components of the **Data Source** pane so that you can understand its core capabilities:

1. **Connections**: This shows what data connections were used. In this case, it shows **Sample – Superstore**; underneath, we can see the name of its source – that is, **Microsoft Excel**. From there, additional data sources can be added or linked.

2. **Use Data Interpreter**: This displays if the data source comes from Excel, CSV, PDF, or Google Sheets. It analyzes the data at its source and cleans it up for data analysis in Tableau. For more information on this helpful built-in tool, please refer to `https://help.tableau.com/current/pro/desktop/en-us/data_interpreter.htm`.

3. **Sheets**: In this example, **Orders**, **People**, and **Returns** show up twice with different icons. In this case, it is showing that the data is coming in from **Sample – Superstore** as tables (the top three) and named ranges (the bottom three). For more on named ranges, please access Tableau's help article at `https://help.tableau.com/current/pro/desktop/en-us/examples_excel.htm#:~:text=Both%20the%20named%20range%20and,and%20then%20selecting%20Insert%20%3E%20Table.`

4. **New Union**: This is a clickable resource that allows a user to create data unions manually or automatically by simply dragging tables into the popup it generates. A **union** is not to be confused with a join. A union is a data source that contains the same fields as another source and is used to append the data rather than define a join relationship.

5. **Data Model**: This shows how data sources are connected. In this example, **Relationships** is being used. It is a model that's been designed and enhanced for use in Tableau. For Tableau's purposes, it is a much more flexible and dynamic smart model. Although joins are still supported, when possible, it is suggested that relationships be used. For more information on relationships and relationships versus joins, please read this help section by Tableau: `https://help.tableau.com/current/pro/desktop/en-us/relate_tables.htm`.

6. **Connection**: This indicates whether the connection is **Live** or **Extract**. By default, data comes in live, but can be extracted so that it can work with static point-in-time data. Its performance can be improved by manual or automated data refreshes.

7. **Filters**: For users utilizing Tableau Online or Tableau Server, data source filters are a way to reduce visible data when you're creating a visualization. This is unlike worksheet filters (which will be explained in future chapters) as it is the most powerful filter that can be utilized from within Tableau Desktop.

8. **Data preview section**: In the preceding example, the **Orders** table is displayed. Apart from being able to preview the number of fields and rows, you can also preview the data type, field name, where the physical table is coming from, and the remote field name (bottom left-hand side).

> **Note**
>
> The remote field name is important for determining what the original name of the field is if it's modified from the original data source in Tableau Desktop. To the immediate right, you can see the fields in the sample table format.
>
> The number of rows revealed can be updated in the top right-hand corner of the data preview (point number 8) section (where it shows **100** rows).

Formatting fields in the Data Source pane

Tableau Desktop provides an effective basic data-cleaning tool. Since the focus of this book is Tableau Desktop, it is important to understand the basics of utilizing the **Data Source** pane's data cleaning functions. Let's cover the basics of what can be done from the **Data Source** pane with the help of the following screenshot:

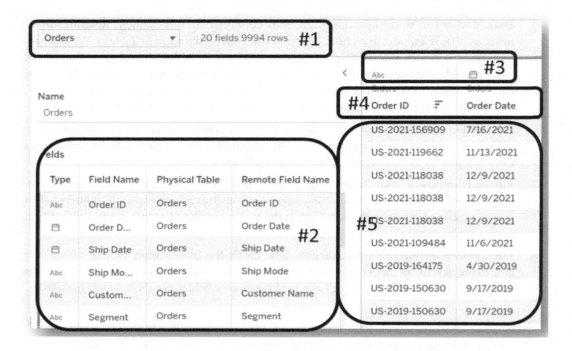

Figure 2.7 – Data Source pane view

Let's understand the highlighted fields:

1. This is the table identifier. To its right, we can see the number of fields (or columns) and the number of rows. Using the dropdown provided, you can access information about other tables in the model.

2. This section displays the data's **Type**, **Field Name**, **Physical Table** (see **Orders** from **Orders**), and **Remote Field Name**.

3. This section shows the data type indicators. Date type updates are often made on this pane (although this can be done using section *#2* and a worksheet).

> **Tip**
>
> Always use section *#3* or a worksheet to update field names. Since Tableau is inherently very good at identifying data types, it may signal there is an error in the data source, so reviewing the data is essential before updating fields. For example, there may be situations where a numerical field has **N/A** instead of a blank or null. That **N/A** will make a numerical field a string because there is a non-numeric component in that field.

4. This section displays the field name and sorting functionality (basic ascending and descending) from the data pane. In section #2, no data is displayed, so this provides an opportunity to have a glance at the data.

5. This section provides sample data for the fields displayed in section #4. From here, you can review and verify the data type before working on the data.

Now that you have a basic understanding of the **Data Source** pane, in the next section, we will cover the data cleaning functionalities available within it.

Core cleaning functions of the Data Source pane

Data rarely comes in perfect shape, even if the data source(s) come in relatively clean. Often, you will need to perform additional manipulation to get it to work as expected. Some of this cleanup can be done right in the Tableau Desktop application. This section covers the best use cases for in-tool cleaning.

Figure 2.8 shows an example of right-clicking to show the available modifications that could potentially be made to a field:

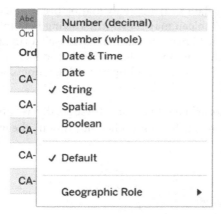

Figure 2.8 – Data type modification options

As shown in *Figure 2.8*, many updates are available when right-clicking on the field. The following list shows some of those updates:

- **Number (decimal)**: For example, 2.32
- **Number (whole)**: For example, 2
- **Date & Time**: For example, 05/22/2022 12:45:02

- **Date**: For example, 05/22/2022

- **String**: A text field

- **Spatial**: Geography

- **Boolean**: A true/false field

- **Geographic Role**: Many of the roles are covered in Tableau's help documentation: `https://` `help.tableau.com/current/pro/desktop/en-us/maps_geographicroles.` `htm`

> **Note**
>
> Tableau denotes what the field is currently. As seen in *Figure 2.8*, Tableau identifies the field as a **String** and notes that the selection was a **Default** selection from Tableau.

> **Caution**
>
> Make sure the date field's data is in a date format before modifying it. When changing a dimension to a measure, Tableau may transform a string field into a number field but will put (**count**) following the field name because the field isn't formatted correctly and includes one or more strings instead of numbers. Most fields that contain incorrect data will appear as strings. For example, a date field may show up as a string if non-date values have been added.

The following screenshot shows field modifications. These are different from data type transformations as they detail how a field can update but don't inherently modify the underlying data types:

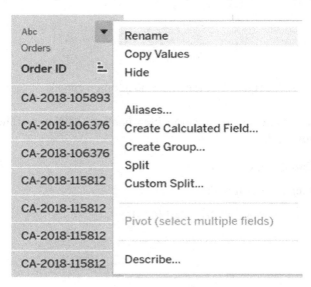

Figure 2.9 – Data pane transformations

As shown in *Figure 2.9*, although Tableau is a data visualization tool, it does offer a wide range of options to clean and shape your data. Note that the following list shows the options for a **String** field; other fields have different options:

- **Rename**: This option allows you to rename a field. Often, fields come in with names that are difficult to understand. This way, you can change the name of a field for ease of understanding, which would also help your end users.

- **Copy Values**: This option stores the field name and sample rows (this defaults to 100, but it can be modified) to a clipboard.

- **Hide**: This option makes the field and its data invisible from a worksheet. This is helpful when you know that a field won't be helpful to end users but comes from the data.

- **Split**: Tableau looks at the data and creates a split based on what it sees and creates default splits (which appear as appended fields). You will need to verify whether you want Tableau to do this as it only looks at the most obvious split scenarios. For total control and predictable splits, you will need to use the **Custom Split…** option, which is covered next.

- **Custom Split…**: With this option, you have the power to determine which character should split up the field (for example, a comma or a dash).

- **Aliases…**: This is not a transformative field, but rather identifies if the field has an alias (similar to point *2* in *Figure 2.8*).

- The other options that are listed are better served on a worksheet and will be covered in *Chapter 3, How to Interpret the Data in a Visualization*:

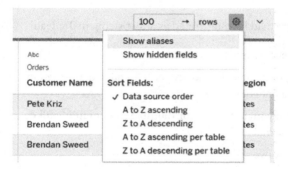

Figure 2.10 – Additional parts of the Data pane

At the top right-hand corner of the **Data** pane is a robust search and sort item. As shown in *Figure 2.10*, by default, **100** rows are displayed. It also provides us with a way to show field aliases and hidden fields with a single click, with some additional sorting functionality.

Summary

In this chapter, you learned how Tableau ingests data sources, cleans up the data types and fields in the **Data Source** pane, and what impacts those modifications have. Working from the **Data** pane and making sure the data is prepared for data visualization is a fundamental building block to enable data visualization itself.

In the next chapter, we will go beyond the **Data Source** pane and learn about the basics of the **Worksheet** tab, where we will begin working with a simple chart for reference purposes.

Knowledge check

1. Why does tall data generally work better in data visualizations? (Select all that apply)

    A. *Fewer null values*

    B. *Charting flexibility*

    C. More data columns or fields

    D. All of the above

2. To quickly scan the number of fields (or columns) and rows in your table, a developer can review the **Data** pane and see a count of each.

    A. *True*

    B. False

3. Why would a date field be interpreted as a text string in Tableau?

    A. *Tableau cannot recognize date fields*

    B. A text string is the default field property for all data ingested in Tableau and always requires a change to a date data type

    C. A text field may include a row or multiple rows of non-null data text that is not consistent with a date format

    D. None of the above

3

How to Interpret Data in a Tableau Visualization

To develop data visualizations and understand the basics, you need to know what to look for in data visualization. Knowing this will not only help you pass the Tableau Desktop Specialist Exam but will also help you and your end users become data fluent.

A primary data visualization key is simplifying complex data to absorbable and actionable insights. Tableau is an incredibly powerful tool for promoting data literacy when wielded appropriately.

In this chapter, we will introduce you to data visualizations in Tableau. There are many components to creating effective data visualizations and you need to be able to define those pieces to tackle the test's second domain, that is, exploring and analyzing data. This domain accounts for 35% of the exam's content. As we build your knowledge with the remainder of the book, fundamental building blocks of that content begin here by exploring the pieces in Tableau that drive each topic.

In this chapter, we will discuss the following topics:

- Simple one-chart data visualization
- Formatting
- Filters and actions
- Visualization tooltips

Technical requirements

You will need one of the following to apply hands-on learning to the chapter's text:

- A Tableau Desktop application. Most versions will work with the exam, but for best results, use 2021.1 or more recent. The location of current downloads is here: `https://www.tableau.com/products/desktop/download`. This version is not free but has a two-week trial.

- A version that meets all the functionality needs of Tableau Desktop but is absolutely free is Tableau Public. It doesn't have all the data and extension functionality that the Tableau Desktop application has, but it has everything you need for the Tableau Desktop Certification. It is available here: `https://public.tableau.com/en-us/s/download`. If it's already downloaded, please use version 2021.1 or later.

- The Superstore Sales dataset. It comes with the Tableau Desktop application automatically, but can also be pulled into the Tableau Public application by downloading it from Tableau Resources here: `https://public.tableau.com/en-us/s/resources?qt-overview_resources=1#qt-overview_resources`.

Let's begin!

Simple one-chart data visualization

In this section, you will be able to see a simple data visualization in Tableau to see how it appears on a sheet. This is a common example, looking at sales. Before working with the tool, it's essential to see an output to better understand charting in data visualization. Beyond that, it will be broken down further to help you rebuild exactly what you see. The chart in *Figure 3.1* is a stacked bar chart that can be made from **Show Me** covered in *Chapter 1* – that chart will also be broken down and developed without **Show Me** in *Chapter 7*.

Seeing a visualization, rather than just describing it in words, supplies the necessary context for understanding. The following figure shows a basic screenshot of a stacked bar chart using the Superstore Sales dataset:

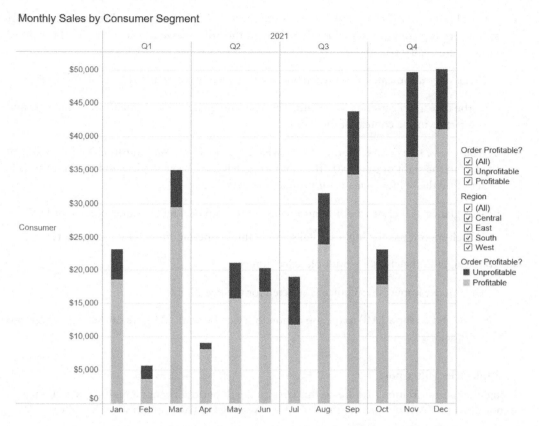

Figure 3.1 – A one-chart visualization example from the Superstore Sales dataset

The chart in *Figure 3.1* is an example of a stacked bar chart. So, what is covered in this chart?

- A specific segment was selected for consumers. Although the segment was selected via a filter, the developer determined not to show the filter for the consumer segment to the end user as that is the only segment needed.

Tip

When developing a dashboard in Tableau, you can decide what filters to reveal to the end user.

- On the *y* axis, dollar amounts can be seen to the right of the **Consumer** header. Since the title says **Sales**, it can be concluded that the dollar amount relates to sales in dollars (USD) (this can be updated to any currency depending on your needs – USD is being used here).

- On the bottom of the chart and the top of the chart, it shows date points. We see the year 2021 at the very top, and quarters directly below. At the bottom, we can see that the abbreviated months are displayed.

  - What does it indicate to you when you see that each month has a representative bar?

    - The date aggregation is by month. The year and quarter are visible to show the year and quarters in the context of the month.

- The bars have two colors. We only know what the colors represent in this chart by looking at the key to the right of the chart. The key shows that the darker shade stands for unprofitable orders, and the lighter shade is for profitable orders.

  - At a glance, is it clear whether more sales come from profitable or unprofitable orders?

  - Which month has the highest total sales? If this is unclear, how can we add clarity?

- To the right of the chart are multiple select filters.

  - How do we know every choice is selected for the two filters?

    - Both filters show (**All**) as the top option to select. Beneath (**All**), we can see that all options are selected.

> **Multiple-select filter note**
> Using filter customizations, (more on this later), a developer can change a multiple-select filter to not show the (**All**) option, but the default is revealing the (**All**) option with that filter.

You built this chart to answer a couple of questions, as our stakeholders wanted to see sales by whether an order was profitable, and wanted to be able to make it selectable by region. You answered those questions with a simple visualization with default formatting. You are now ready to turn to your stakeholders for feedback.

Formatting a chart in Tableau

Formatting capabilities of data visualization are what helps separate Tableau from many tools. For basic formatting, the goal is to help supply additional information to help with stakeholder insights. You will be able to push past default chart building and create something instinctively engaging. Users don't want to spend a lot of time finding basic answers to a question or have too much information shown, making it hard to find relevant data points.

After sharing the preceding version of the dashboard with stakeholders, they make a few requests to make it easier to understand and see what they want to see, as follows:

1. We know we are looking at the whole of 2021, so we just want to see the months on the bottom.

2. We want to see the values on the bar in thousands and do not need the full dollar amount.

3. Since we know we are looking at the Consumer segment, is there any way to remove it from this chart and just keep it in the title? Can we also remove the sales axis if we can see the number on the chart?

4. Can we make the bars a little wider?

5. Can we add the value in thousands to the bars?

6. Can we change the font to a more accessible font, such as Verdana?

7. Please remove gridlines from the visualization.

8. Can we see the unprofitable orders at the bottom instead of profitable ones? It will help us see the impact of unprofitable orders more easily.

You can tell your stakeholders were positive about the visualization but ended up with eight iterative requests. The good news is, these formatting requests are quite simple to apply in Tableau:

*   For the first point, we just needed to remove the dimensional date fields for Year and Quarter. The top section was removed, and it also helped with the omission of many vertical lines (see *Figure 3.2*):

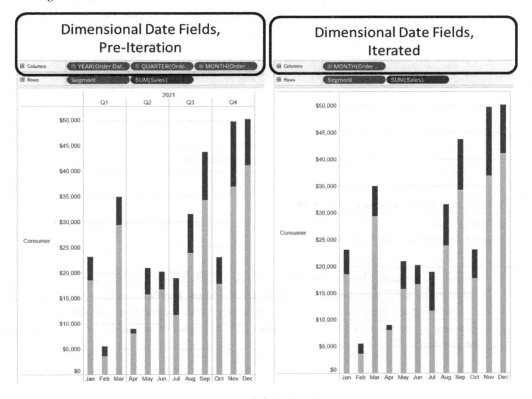

Figure 3.2 – Solving iteration 1

- For the second request, we are required to modify the number formatting. First, we need to determine where the numbers come from and show them on the chart. We see the only measure is sales and recognize that's what we are measuring. In the second part of this iteration, we need to edit both the **Axis** tab and the **Pane** tab. To format a field in Tableau, simply right-click the pill and select **Format** (see *Figure 3.3*); this will allow you access to both **Axis** and **Pane** formatting. From there, many options appear. Since we have already labeled currency, all we need to do is select **Currency (Custom)**, remove the decimal places, and select **Display Units | Thousands (K)** (see *Figure 3.3*):

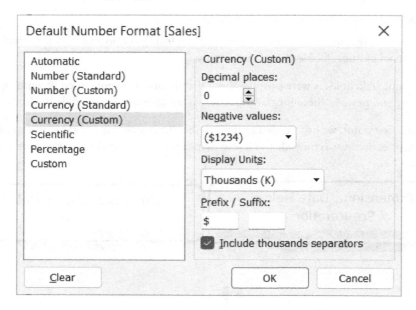

Figure 3.3 – Number formatting for iteration 2

> **More on number formatting in Tableau**
> https://help.tableau.com/current/pro/desktop/en-us/formatting_specific_numbers.htm

- Showing and hiding headers in Tableau is remarkably simple. All you need to do is right-click on the fields with headers and uncheck the **Show Header** checkbox (see *Figure 3.4*). Considering the items here show up on the *y* axis, we know and can see values on the rows showing up on the *x* axis because the rows only have two values, and they are represented on the chart:

Figure 3.4 – Hiding headers from iteration 3

- The fourth iteration does not require special formatting or new fields. To increase the width of the dimensional bars, go to the **Marks** card and adjust the slider (as seen in *Figure 3.5*):

Figure 3.5 – Sizing from the Marks section for iteration 4

- The fifth iteration is another simple execution in the **Marks** section. Since we have changed the format of the currency, we will simply select **Label** and then check **Show Label**. When selecting **Show mark labels**, the text will default to show **(SUM) Sales** as that is the measure being shown. In this case, the value of **$##,###** was modified to **$##K**:

Figure 3.6 – Example of selecting Labels and checking Show mark labels for iteration 5

More on formatting field labels

https://help.tableau.com/current/pro/desktop/en-us/viewparts_
marks_markproperties.htm

- Since we are working on a worksheet, we can define all the fonts at a workbook level. This is another simple adjustment in Tableau. At the top of the worksheet, select **Format** and then **Font**. This will show the font at the worksheet level. Changing the font to **Default** in the **Worksheet** section will update that font for all pieces of the dashboard by default unless overridden when updating other fields below the worksheet level:

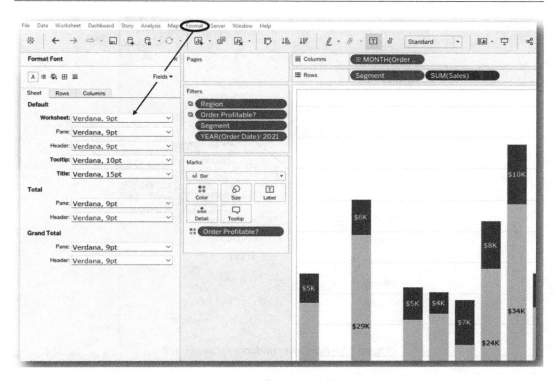

Figure 3.7 – Verdana font override for iteration 6

- Removing gridlines is quite a common update and fortunately easy in Tableau. Since we removed headers, gridlines in the visual don't help insight. Go to **Format** and then **Lines**. Once you're there, check **Sheet**, **Rows**, and **Columns** (even if the **Sheet** section shows **None**, there may be gridlines in the rows or columns that also need to be selected as **None**). In this example, we removed the gridlines displayed in **Rows** by selecting the **None** option (see *Figure 3.8*):

More formatting at the worksheet level including lines

```
https://help.tableau.com/current/pro/desktop/en-us/formatting_
worksheet.htm
```

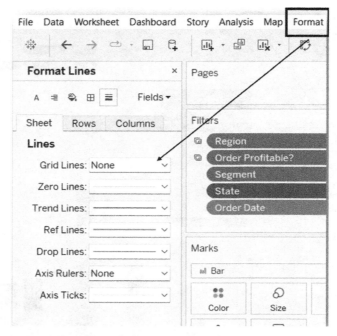

Figure 3.8 – Removing gridlines for iteration 7

- There are many ways to flip dimensions to show a new dimension at the bottom or in a new order, and some will be shown in future chapters. The simplest way to do this with a small number of dimensions is to simply drag from the legend to the place you want it. In this example, we dragged **Unprofitable** from the top to the bottom, which the chart mirrors (unless there is a primary sort from a parent field that overrides it). Also, the sorted field, in this case **Order Profitable**, will display a sort icon in its pill (on the right). See *Figure 3.9* for the reference and appearance:

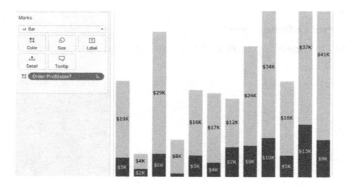

Figure 3.9 – Changing the order of a dimension for iteration 8

After you have developed these updates (see *Figure 3.9*), the iterations will enhance the stakeholders' experience. They will be quite impressed to get a new dashboard to review and see their requests applied.

Monthly Sales by Consumer Segment

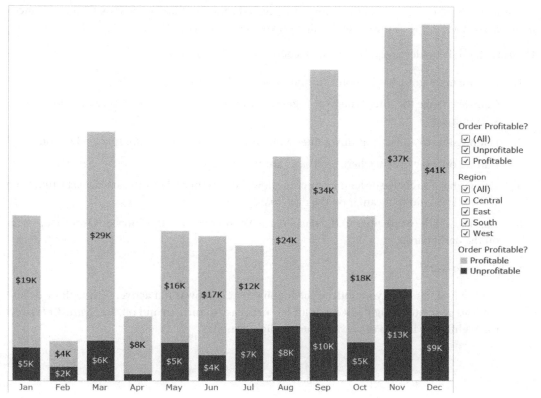

Figure 3.10 – Iterated dashboard

We have covered iterations related to formatting. Now the stakeholders have suggestions for enhancing the interactivity of the visualization, and we will check this out in the next section.

Filters and actions

Here is where the magic of Tableau comes into play. In this section, you will learn about standard filters and actions. We will iterate once again because a stakeholder with some familiarity with the tool wants to be able to highlight the color marks and add another filter to the visual. More advanced filtering, such as adding to the context, will be covered in *Chapter 7*.

Here are the stakeholder's requests for the second round of iterations:

1. Can we highlight what is profitable and unprofitable on the chart?
2. Can we change the filter type to a single select for the region and also have the capability of selecting **All**?
3. Is it possible to add a drop-down filter with only relevant states for the specified region?
4. Can we only see orders where total sales are at least $20?
5. Can we have a relative order date filter to show the current and prior years' data starting from 1/1/2021? We do not want it on the dashboard.
6. Can we add the **State** filter to the dashboard? We do not want the **Sales** or **Order Date** filter on the dashboard.

Now, let's get to work!

1. On the first iteration, you noticed the highlighter action was not active. Although by default Tableau generates a highlight for color keys, it's easy to turn on and off. In *Figure 3.11*, select the highlighter icon to re-activate the highlight action:

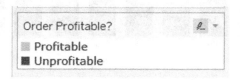

Figure 3.11 – Order Profitable highlighter

Testing the highlighter is as easy as selecting an item in the color key. In *Figure 3.12*, we have selected **Unprofitable** to verify that the highlighter is active:

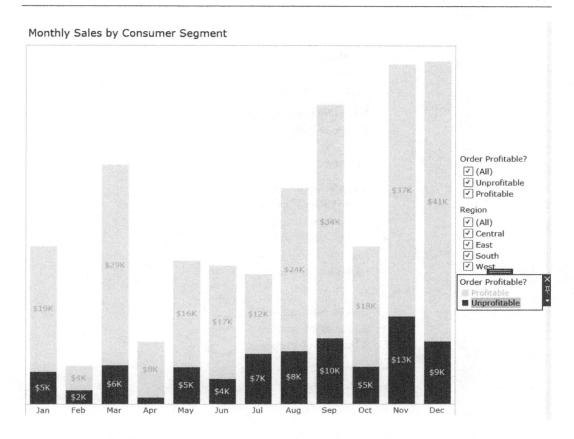

Figure 3.12 – Highlighter verification (Unprofitable orders highlighted for iteration 1 in round 2)

2. In Tableau, you have a lot of flexibility with filters. In this case, we will use the filter edit to modify the filter type to be able to select one region at a time or all of them.

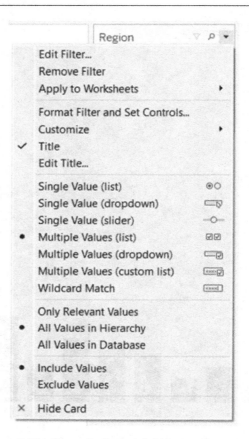

Figure 3.13 – Filter edit (Region field (string dimension))

By applying this, the **Single Value (list)** filter will transform from a multiple check filter to a radio button filter, as shown in *Figure 3.14*:

Monthly Sales by Consumer Segment

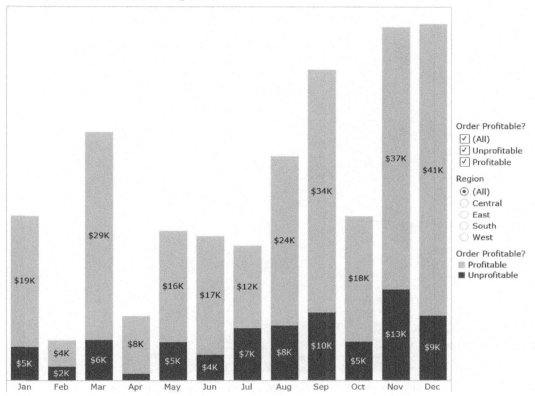

Figure 3.14 – Single selection filter for iteration 2 in round 2

3. To show relevant states in a drop-down filter, we need to tackle this request in several steps, as follows:

    I.   Add **State** to the filter.

    II. Select **Use all** to show all results (see *Figure 3.15*) – this will make it easier to work with.

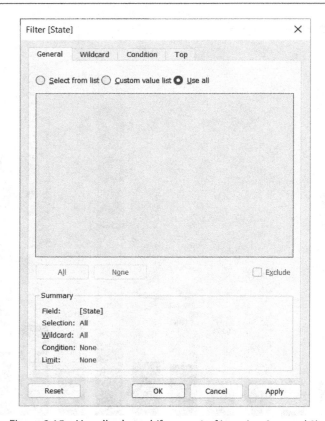

Figure 3.15 – Use all selected (for part 1 of iteration 3, round 2)

III.   Select **Show Filter** from the **State** filter section to begin editing it in the sheet (see *Figure 3.16*):

Figure 3.16 – Show Filter option selected (for part 2 of iteration 3, round 2)

IV.   In the filter selection of the sheet, select the arrow and change the filter type to **Multiple Values (dropdown)**. The filter will change from one large checkbox list to a compact multiple-selection list. The section will close; select the carrot again and then select **Only Relevant Values**. For both, see *Figure 3.17*. These options are selected so that values do not take up a lot of dashboard space. Also, selecting relevant values will restrict the size of the list further by order profitability and regions selected. Usually, when filters are selected, users want to see options available based on the selection:

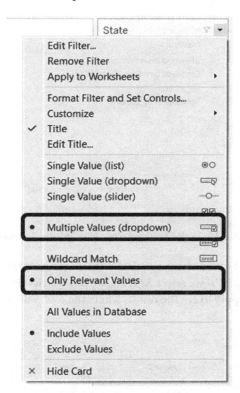

Figure 3.16 – Multiple Values (dropdown) and Only Relevant Values
selected for the State field (for part 3 of iteration 3, round 2)

4.   For the fourth iteration, we will need to use a new filter type. This is a measures filter, so the options are different. If you drag in the **Sales** field, you can view the new selections:

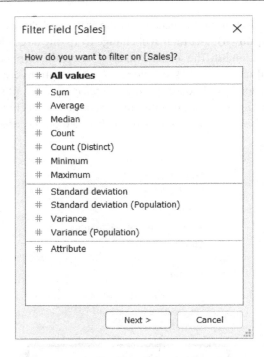

Figure 3.18 – Sales field measure filter (round 2, iteration 4)

No changes need to be made here, so select **Next**. In the next section, we can limit to **At least**, as shown in *Figure 3.19*. If we select **At least**, we can restrict the sales to at least $20 by typing in 2 0. Now select **Apply** to see the results where the total sales are at least $20:

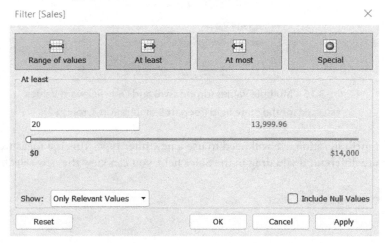

Figure 3.19 – Using At least in a measures filter via the Sales field (round 2, iteration 4)

5. To get the dates to automatically show the current and prior year, a **Relative Date** filter needs to be added (see *Figure 3.20*):

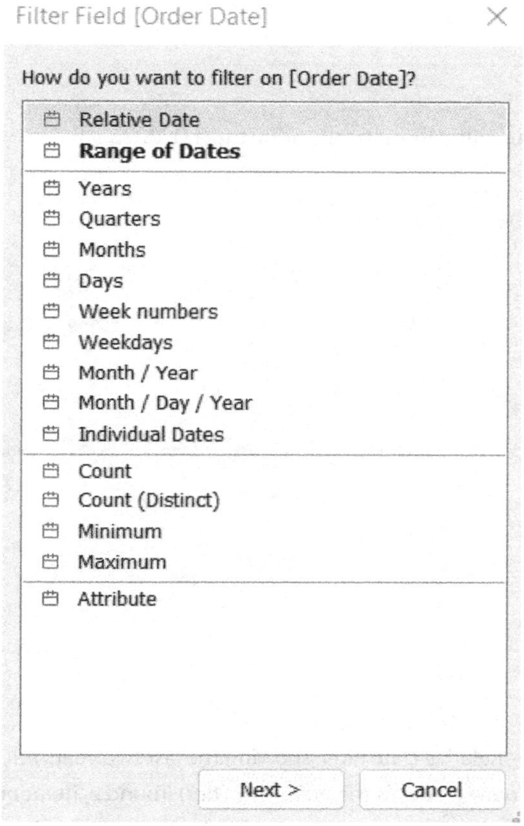

Figure 3.20 – Date filter with Relative Date selected (round 2, iteration 5)

Tableau makes it simple to automate the date as it is by default anchored to today's date. Since the stakeholder asked for the last two calendar years of data, selecting **Years** and typing 2 in the **Last N years** section will change the dates beginning with **1/1/2021** (see *Figure 3.21*). To finalize the date automation, select **Apply**:

> **Note**
> As of 1/1/2023, the date will automatically adjust to 1/1/2022.

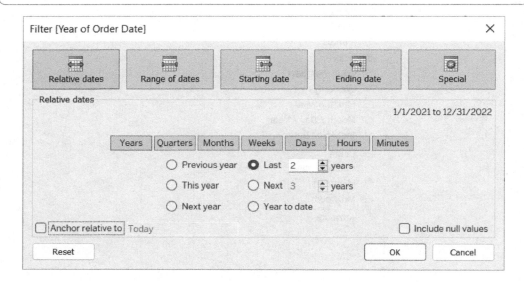

Figure 3.21 – Relative Date filter, showing the last two years Anchor relative
to Today (Today is the default anchor) (round 2, iteration 5)

6.   Finally, we need to put this all together. Since we have the sheet on our dashboard, these filters will not automatically appear; we need to call them. To do that, we need to select the sheet on the dashboard. Go to **Analysis**, and then select **Filters**, then select **State** to show the **State** filter on the dashboard:

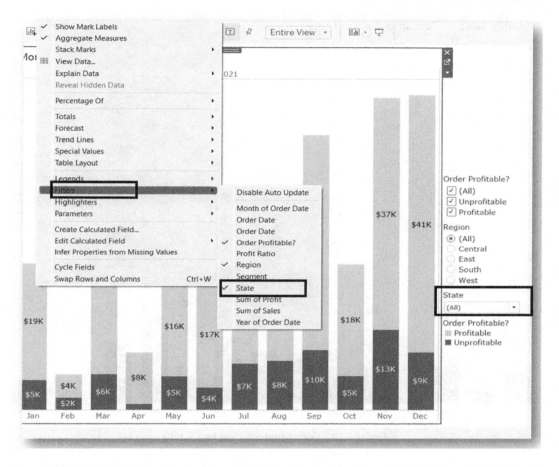

Figure 3.22 – Selecting a filter on a dashboard and adjusting the filter format for State (round 2, iteration 6)

Once selected, it will pop into a space. Unfortunately, the filters only appear with the default settings, and updating it will need to be done again at the dashboard level.

> **Tip**
>
> Although the iteration requests of updating the dashboard only need to be done at the dashboard level, it's worthwhile testing on the sheet before bringing it out to the dashboard to verify everything works as expected at the sheet level. This will come into play when a dashboard includes more than one sheet. A deeper dive into dashboard formatting will be covered in *Chapter 8*.

After adjusting the filters and their layout on the right side, here is the completion of our round 2 iteration:

Monthly Sales by Consumer Segment

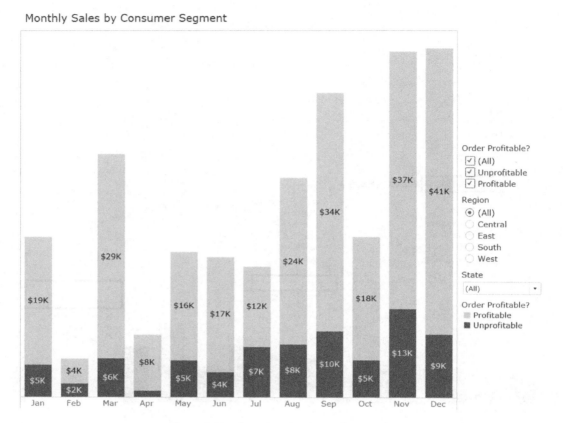

Figure 3.23 – Completed iteration for round 2

> **Additional resources on actions (from Tableau)**
> https://help.tableau.com/current/pro/desktop/en-us/actions.htm
> https://help.tableau.com/current/pro/desktop/en-us/filtering.htm

The stakeholders worked with the dashboard some more and want to see further information when hovering over the bars. We will cover the final round of iterations in the *Tooltips* section.

Tooltips

Tooltips on visualizations are a window to added context. They help users navigate further into the data and capture more insight. Tooltips appear by default on visualizations when hovering over a data point. However, the default model is not organized in a way that tells a story.

Your current dashboard will have tooltips that look something like this:

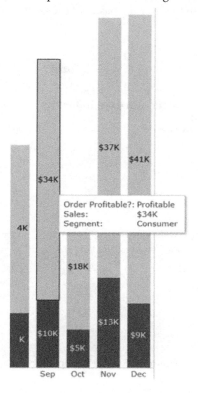

Figure 3.24 – Default tooltips

The default tooltips are okay, but the stakeholders want a way to make the information more narrative and useful. Tooltips can be edited in many ways. Besides being able to add dynamic results of dimensions, measures, or parameters when bringing in those fields, there are a host of text edits that can be made.

In our final round of iterations, you will have more requests to implement. Here are those requests. The good news is that the data is already included, and there are no calculations needed. In *Chapter 5*, you will learn about calculations and their syntax in Tableau for many types of functions.

Here are the requests of the stakeholder for the third round of iterations:

1. Add the year to the visualization to show the year and month, and add both to the tooltip.
2. Is it possible to add profit per order and profit ratio to the tooltip?
3. Can you bold all results from dynamic fields?
4. Can we change the format to a sentence structure rather than a list?

Before you start working on the rest of these iterations, it's important to know which tools are available in tooltips – *Figure 3.25* will begin to cover the basics of the tooltip editor:

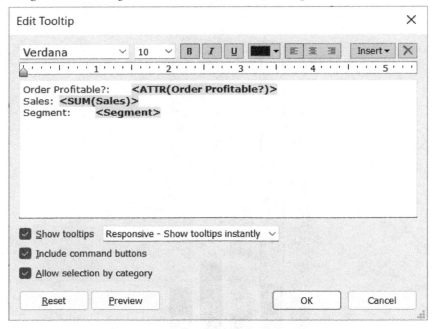

Figure 3.25 – The tooltip editor

The top part (until the Insert dropdown) is the standard text editor. From there, you can change the font and font size; bold, italicize, and underline the text; change the font color; and left align, center align, or right align the text.

> **Notes**
> Tableau does not have spell check or justify alignment functionality.

The **Insert** section is a robust collection of additional items that can be added to the tooltip. Most commonly, you can add a sheet (usually done to support a Viz in Tooltip), a **Data Update Time**, and any parameters or fields associated with the impacted visualization.

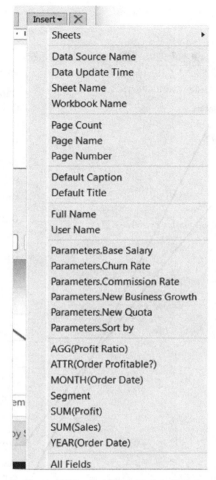

Figure 3.26 – Tooltip Insert actions

Now that you are familiar with the tooltip editor, let us begin incorporating the stakeholders' requests:

1. Applying the first iteration requires an update to the visualization. You need to add **Order Date** to **Columns** and select the year of **Order Date** dimension (see *Figure 3.27*). The year will appear at the top and will not combine months if there are multiple years.

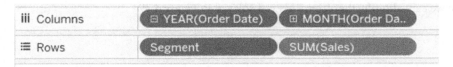

Figure 3.27 – Adding YEAR(Order Date) to Columns (round 3, iteration 1)

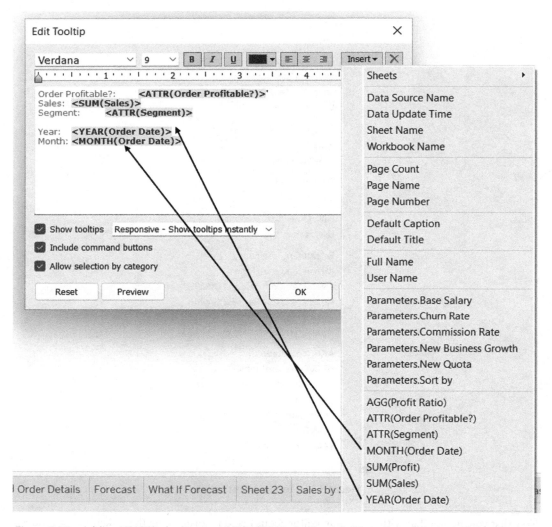

Figure 3.28 – Adding YEAR(Order Date) and MONTH (Order Date) fields to the tooltip (round 3, iteration 1)

Pro tip

When adding a field, it's best practice to include a static field identifier in front of it to make sure we can edit it further later. This is displayed in *Figure 3.29*.

2. For the next request, you do not want to change the visualization, but add context to it. Fortunately, Tableau has a section committed to this. All we need to do is drag the required fields to the tooltip, add them to the tooltip (see *Figure 3.28*), and verify the format. In *Figure 3.29*, I added static labels (or text that is not dynamic) in front of the variable field values (which can be seen as Tableau provides a highlight over those fields):

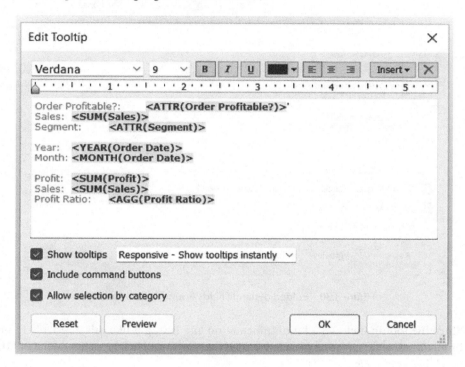

Figure 3.29 – Adding Profit and Profit Ratio plus static fields in front of
iteration 1 and 2 to add context (round 3, iteration 2)

3. All dynamic fields need to be made bold so users can see the valuable information. To do that, we need to select each of the highlights and select the **B** button in the editing space (see *Figure 3.30*):

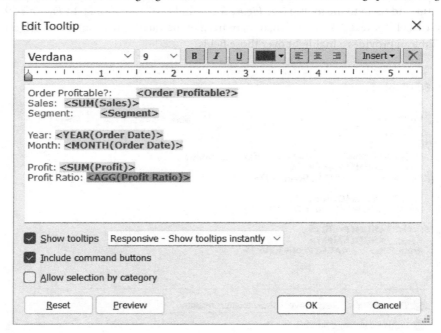

Figure 3.30 – Bolded dynamic fields (round 3, iteration 3)

4. Since the tooltip includes a lot of information and listing it like this doesn't help provide immediate insight, creating a narrative with the tooltip will help people understand the text much better (see *Figure 3.31*):

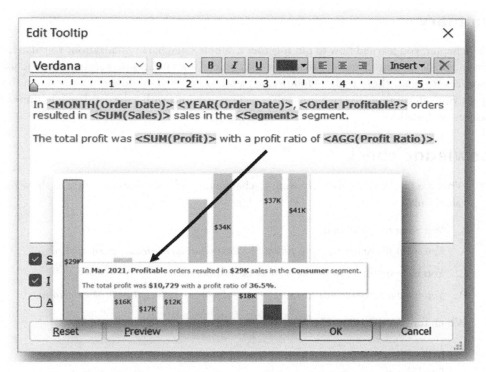

Figure 3.31 – Tooltip narrative updates to display insights from dynamic field
values when hovering over March 2021 (round 3, iteration 4)

With clean narrative tooltips and some dynamic text options, stakeholders will be able to see, with
much more clarity, what each data point represents.

Additional resources on tooltips
```
https://help.tableau.com/current/pro/desktop/en-us/view_parts.
htm#Tooltips
```

Summary

In this chapter, you learned how to put together a simple one-chart visualization. You also learned about and made iterative changes to that chart with general formatting, filters and actions, and tooltips. The process to make those updates followed a pattern of real-world iteration requests. In the next chapter, you will continue to learn how to create visualizations with a deeper dive into dimensions, measures, and marks.

Knowledge check

1. What are two reasons you may want to change the default values in a filter to show relevant values only?

    A. You want to see all data.

    B. *You want to see the data pre-filtered by filters that have already been applied.*

    C. You have no filters in the worksheet or dashboard.

    D. *You have a lot of records to select from and want to reduce the visible selections.*

2. Which functionality does the text editor natively include (select all that apply)?

    A. *Font selection.*

    B. Spell check.

    C. *Font coloring.*

    D. *Center alignment.*

    E. *Inserting different sheets.*

3. What is the default anchor date when using a relative date filter?

    A. The date the visualization was made.

    B. The date the last data came in.

    C. *Today's date.*

    D. None of the above.

4

Working with Dimensions, Measures, and Marks (Oh My)

Building any data visualization in Tableau requires knowledge of data dimensions, data measures, and working with the **Marks** card. Understanding how they work together to display your data provides you with a significant Tableau skill base to further develop as a practitioner. In addition, working with dimensions and marks is pertinent for examining **Sharing Insights (Domain 3)** and **Understanding Tableau Concepts (Domain 4)**.

In this chapter, you will learn about data dimensions, data measures, the usage of discrete versus continuous fields, working with the **Mark** card, and being able to apply these concepts to understand how to create various visualizations. This is foundational knowledge necessary to master concepts required for the examination and to give you a deeper understanding so that you are effectively able to answer knowledge-based questions.

In this chapter, we will cover the following topics:

- Grasping data dimensions
- Data measures
- Discrete versus continuous
- The Tableau Marks section

Technical requirements

You will need one of the following for hands-on learning with this chapter's text:

- The Tableau Desktop application. Most versions will work with the exam, but for best results, use 2021.1 or later. The location of current downloads is https://www.tableau.com/products/desktop/download. This version is not free but has a 2-week trial.

- A version with similar functionality to Tableau Desktop but is free is Tableau Public. It does not have all the data and extension functionality of the Tableau Desktop application, but it has everything you need for the Tableau Desktop Specialist certification. It is available here: `https://public.tableau.com/en-us/s/download`. If downloaded already, please use version 2021.1 or later.

- The Superstore sales dataset. It automatically comes with the Tableau Desktop application but can also be pulled into the Tableau Public application by downloading it from Tableau resources here: `https://public.tableau.com/en-us/s/resources?qt-overview_resources=1#qt-overview_resources`.

Grasping data dimensions

In the data dimensions section, we will look at data dimensions in the Superstore dataset to understand each one, how they can be used, and what they represent.

In *Figure 4.1*, you can see a snapshot of various data dimensions in one view:

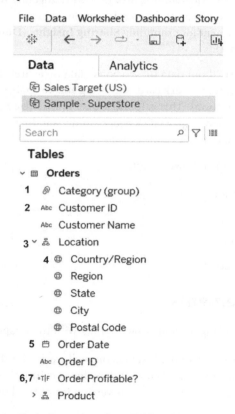

Figure 4.1 – Data dimensions from Tableau's Superstore dataset

As you can see, there are many items to consider when working with data dimensions. The following list breaks down the necessary components:

1. **Group**: You can create groups for a single data dimension field. Groups are created manually and are identified by a paperclip in front of a field name. More information on creating and manipulating groups will be covered in *Chapter 7*.

Important group note

Groups can only be made with data dimensions and not data measures.

---

2. **String dimensions**: String dimensions include an **Abc** identifier. They contain qualitative data that helps define the level of data aggregation or provides additional data context.

3. **Hierarchies**: Multiple fields can be put into a hierarchy. For example, in *Figure 4.1*, **Location** is the hierarchy for the indented fields beneath it. More information on creating and manipulating hierarchies will be covered in *Chapter 7*.

Important hierarchy note

Hierarchies can only be made with data dimensions and not data measures, as Tableau only recognizes dimensional hierarchies.

---

4. **Geographic**: Tableau identifies the **Country/Region**, **Region**, **State**, **City**, and **Postal Code** fields as geographic. Tableau can generate latitude and longitude from these fields when appropriately defined and plot them on a map. More information on working with and assigning geography will be covered in *Chapter 6*.

5. **Date**: **Order Date** is defined as a date field. A calendar icon is assigned to a date field. A calendar with a clock icon represents the date and time fields.

6. **Boolean or true/false fields**: Boolean fields are always dimensional and provide one of two options that may or may not be true or false. For example, in this field, the result will yield **Profitable** if the condition is true and **Unprofitable** if the condition is false, as shown in *Figure 4.2*.

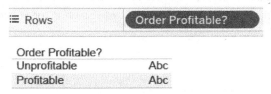

Figure 4.2: Adding Order Profitable? Boolean fields under Rows shows that the
result can be only one of two options (Unprofitable or Profitable)

7. **Calculated field**: In the Boolean field, as shown in *Figure 4.1* (**6**), an equal sign appears in front of it. Calculated fields can be made to identify dimensions or measures. In this case, you want to see whether you can define an order as profitable, but you do not need to see how profitable. However, a dimensional result can be handy to get a glance at how many orders are profitable versus unprofitable.

As demonstrated, dimensions contain many characteristics, providing nearly infinite possibilities to frame data. However, that dataframe will not include a picture of what each dimension truly represents without measures.

Data measures

Data measures provide the meaning behind the context. Measures make it possible to create graphic representations of what data dimensions cover. *Figure 4.3* shows how dimensions and measures are defined in the **Data** section:

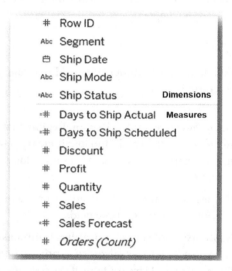

Figure 4.3 – The (faint) line separating dimensions and measures on each table in the Data pane. This snapshot comes from the Orders table in the Superstore dataset

---

> **Important number note**
>
> *Figure 4.3* has a # field called **Row ID**. Although a number field defaults to a measure, it can be converted to a dimension. When converted to a dimension, it cannot be used to measure dimensions but can be converted back to a measure if needed.
>
> Any string or geographic dimension can be converted to a measure, but that measure will be a count distinct from the former dimension. Other dimensional fields such as dates and Boolean cannot be converted to measures (unless a new calculated field is made).

The field representations of measures are always numbers (or the number/pound icon). Like data dimensions, they can come from calculations or data. For example, in Tableau, a count field is generated from the name of the table (or **Orders (Count)**).

> **Row count field note**
>
> In old versions of Tableau (no longer supported), there was a generated field called **Number of Records**. In Version 2020.2 and later, this field was replaced by the **Table (Count)** field. All tables will include this field.

Now that we have grasped dimensions and measures, we need to dive deeper and begin to explore variations of those fields, which can be discrete or continuous.

Discrete versus continuous (blue versus green fields – otherwise known as pills)

The customary rule of thumb is that *measures are green, or continuous,* and *dimensions are blue, or discrete*. In most cases, this is accurate, but measures and dimensions can be both discrete and continuous.

Tableau considers continuous fields as fields with an infinite range that can create an axis for a visualization. On the other hand, discrete fields are finite and are used to build headers for a visualization.

The most common data types in dimensions that see a continuous value are dates. To test which fields can be modified to discrete or continuous, you simply need to right-click the field to see whether it can be converted from discrete to continuous or continuous to discrete. Dimensions that do not permit changes from discrete to continuous or vice versa will not show this option. Please see *Figure 4.4*:

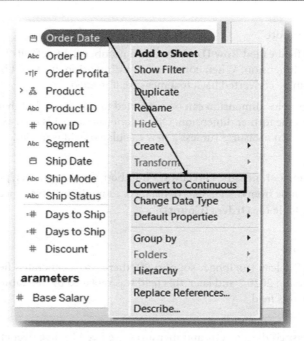

Figure 4.4: Order Date is a discrete dimension but can be converted to a continuous (or green) dimension

The following screenshot shows how changing between a discrete and continuous date field impacts a visualization when counting orders by date for every date in the dataset:

> **Note**
>
> Typically, you would not want to show data for a year using exact dates, but doing so shows the impact of continuous versus discrete dates on a visual.

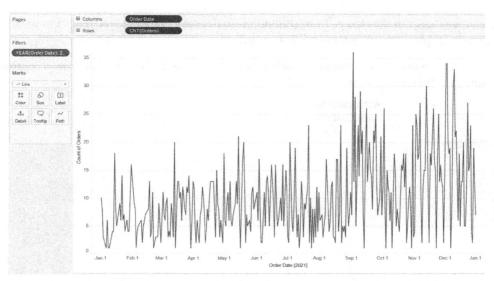

Figure 4.5: The continuous order date filtered for 2021 using the count of orders

In *Figure 4.5*, we see a continuous line of dates, with a fitted axis of dates rolled up by month (for example, **Jan 1**, **Feb 1**, and so on). Let us see what happens when the order date on **Columns** is changed from **Continuous to Discrete**.

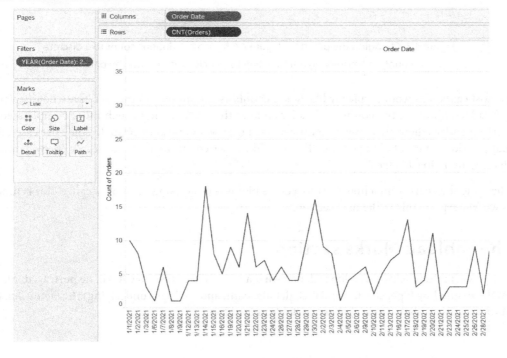

Figure 4.6: The order date changed from continuous to discrete

You can see that with the change from continuous to discrete, every date referenced in the dataset needs to be displayed as a header instead of a fitted axis.

In *Figure 4.7*, we can see what happens when we shift the measure of order count from a continuous measure to a discrete measure:

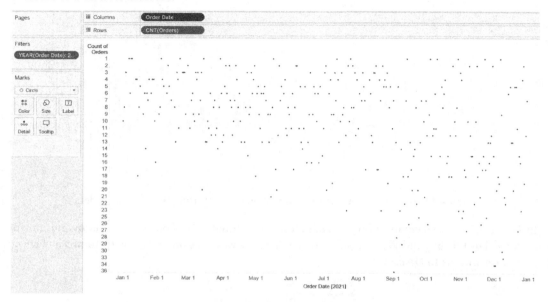

Figure 4.7: Changing the plot from Figure 4.6 from a continuous count to a discrete count and modifying it from a line to a circle plot to show the data

In most cases, you would typically like to see counts as continuous, so the counts are not displayed as headers. Showing the counts as headers makes the visualization much more complicated to comprehend, as there are many dimensions that a user would need to grasp. In some use cases, this may help look at trends, but you usually would like to see counts in one view cleanly. We will discuss charting more in *Chapter 7*.

Changing the chart from a line chart to a circle plot was done using the **Marks** card – this is timely, as we will explore this in the next section.

The Tableau Marks section

In **Marks**, Tableau helps a developer define what a user will see and how it will be portrayed. Marks can be defined by type, color, size, label, details, path, and tooltips (underlying). In *Figure 4.8*, the **Marks** section is shown as it appears on Tableau Desktop:

Figure 4.8: The Marks section in Tableau

The preceding screenshot is just the preliminary hub for transforming a visualization. In *Figure 4.9*, we will show you the options for changing mark types (as of Tableau Version 2022.1).

Tableau mark types

Tableau mark types dictate the framework of a visualization. You can use this to determine the chart type and share how data is displayed on a sheet:

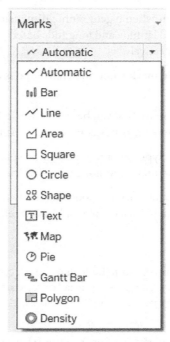

Figure 4.9: The mark type options

Let us briefly explain the mark types covered in the preceding screenshot:

- An **Automatic** or generated mark type in Tableau looks at the data on the visualization and tries to guess how it could be displayed based on its input. In the preceding screenshot, the mark type is **Automatic**, but a line-type symbol is displayed. This symbol means that the type selected was a line mark type.

- The **Bar** type is a mark type that transforms data into a bar chart.

- The **Area** type is a mark type that converts data into an area chart.

- The **Square** type is a mark type that transforms data into a square chart (placing the marks at each data point).

- The **Circle** type is a mark type that converts the data into a circle chart, placing the marks at each defined data point (see *Figure 4.7* to see what that looks like).

- The **Shape** type is a mark type that transforms data into a square chart (placing the marks at each defined data point – it differs from square and circle marks, as different shapes can be displayed dimensionally, whereas with square or circle charts, only a square or circle shape can be used).

- The **Text** type is used in most cases to display data in table format.

- The **Map** type marks a graph when a geographic dimension is added to the **Marks** section. Tableau then adds a generated latitude and longitude based on geographic dimensions to create polygons or data markers effectively.

- The **Pie** type shows an angle mark when the chart type is a pie chart and the data supports that sort of measurement.

- The **Gantt Bar** type is a line mark that can be sized based on a measurement. It is a mark type beneficial for project management, as it becomes a bar sized by the number of days from a date.

- The **Polygon** type is a mark type generally used to fill space. The most common scenario is when Tableau uses it to build maps, but it is often used for complex/bespoke visualizations.

- The **Density** type mark is usually used in coordination with a map in Tableau. Therefore, it is best utilized when many data points are at an address level.

> **Note**
>
> For more explanation and examples from Tableau on mark types, please review this Tableau *Help* article: `https://help.tableau.com/current/pro/desktop/en-us/viewparts_marks_marktypes.htm#ShapeMark`.

Now that we have briefly covered mark types, we can now share ways to further contextualize data by controlling the appearance of marks.

Managing marks' appearance

You have a visualization created but need to add more to it to provide additional context for end users. Tableau offers many ways to control this aspect of data visualization. See *Figure 4.10* on how to manage mark appearances.

Figure 4.10: Marks managing options (labeled 1–6) from Tableau 2022.2

We will work from the preceding numbered sections to detail how marks can be managed from the **Marks** card section:

1. **Color** can be added from discrete fields to add a color per dimension or continuous coloring to provide shading. *Dimensional coloring* means a user needs to define a color per dimension. *Continuous coloring* provides one (sequential coloring) or two options (diverging coloring) that get shaded to fill the lowest to the highest value in the range.

2. **Size** can be used to modify the appearance of data marks in a visualization. Like **Color**, it is used for highlighting data marks.

3. **Label** provides text labels to a visualization to help viewers see values with any charting.

4. **Detail** is used to add detail to a visualization to create additional data marks and dimensionality. It does not change the mark type but impacts the number of data points visible.

5. **Tooltip** is a feature that Tableau provides to extend the understanding of the primary view. Default tooltips show dimensions and measure data brought into a visualization, but they can be modified with additional text and even different sheets of data for supplemental visualizations (often referred to as viz-in-tooltips).

6. The final option is a custom space dependent on the mark type selected. Some visualizations such as maps may not show anything in that spot, but lines and polygons include **Path** management to define where you tell Tableau to connect a line or polygon.

> **Note**
>
> For more explanations and examples from Tableau on managing marks, please review this Tableau *Help* article: `https://help.tableau.com/current/pro/desktop/en-us/viewparts_marks_markproperties.htm`.

As you can see, there is an exhaustive list of context and insight to be added when making updates to marks.

Summary

In this chapter, you learned how Tableau works with data dimensions and data measures, creates visualizations based on mark types, and manipulates mark types. These items allow us to extend our tool capabilities. In addition, you are working toward the Sharing Insights and Understanding Tableau Concepts domains of the exam. Future chapters will dig into even more detail about those core domains. In the next chapter, we will cover the syntax of Tableau functions and their basic calculations.

Knowledge check

1. The following is/are true of number fields (select all that apply):

    A. They can be a data measure

    B. They can be a dimension

    C. They can be a continuous field

    D. They can be a discrete field

2. Discrete fields can be used to build an axis:

    A. True

    B. False

3. Which field type is needed to build a map with Tableau-generated latitude and longitude fields?

    A. Geographic

    B. Numerical

    C. String

    D. Date

    E. None of the preceding

5

Calculations and Functions Syntax

Understanding and working with calculations is required of every Tableau developer. Functions and calculations amplify the magnitude of the data's power. This exam does not require you to be an expert in calculations and functions, but you are required to understand enough to interpret basic calculations from knowledge-based questions. You are likely to know enough to troubleshoot why a calculation does not work. The questions are tricky, so understanding the functions and calculations process will be an essential part of covering Domain 2, which is 35% of the exam's score. This chapter will provide a deeper look at the skills and opportunities for developers to push past the very basics and open up a new world of insights and discovery.

In this chapter, we will cover the following topics:

- Tableau functions

- Creating basic calculations in Tableau

- Introduction to **Level of Detail (LOD)** expressions and parameters

- Order of operations

Technical requirements

You will need the following to learn from this chapter:

- A Tableau Desktop application. Most versions will work with the exam, but for best results, use 2021.1 or more recent. The location of current downloads is `https://www.tableau.com/products/desktop/download`. This version is not free but has a 2-week trial.

- A version that meets all the functionality needs of Tableau Desktop but is free is Tableau Public. It does not have all the data and extension functionality of the Tableau Desktop application, but everything you need for the Tableau Desktop certification. It is available here: `https://`

`public.tableau.com/en-us/s/download`. If you've downloaded it already, please use version 2021.1 or later.

- Superstore Sales dataset. It automatically comes with the Tableau Desktop application but can also be pulled into the Tableau Public application by downloading from *Tableau Resources* here: `https://public.tableau.com/en-us/s/resources?qt-overview_resources=1#qt-overview_resources`.

Let's get started!

Tableau functions

Functions are the options Tableau uses to create **calculations**. Tableau has a robust set of functions for developers to create an almost infinite number of calculations with many capabilities. You will not need to learn all functions at this level as many are used for more advanced applications, but we will cover the foundational functions in the following subsections.

Number functions

Numerical fields or fields with # in front of them can be used in calculations to create or refer to something that can be measured. Number functions can only be applied with numerical fields. The number functions that are most common and will be referenced in the exam appear in the following list:

- ABS: Provides the absolute or non-negative value of a number from the field used. It changes all negative numbers to the positive version of the number and keeps non-negatives the same—for example, `ABS(-10) = 10`.

- MAX: Finds the maximum value of the field (based on filters and dimensions used in a visualization) and provides the highest value. For example, to find whether the `Profit` field contains values from 6,600 to 8,400 in Tableau 2022.1: `MAX([Profit]) = 8,400`.

> **Note**
> There is a MAX function for many function types.

- MIN: Finds the minimum value of the field (based on filters and dimensions used in a visualization) and provides the lowest value. For example, if the `Profit` field contains values from -6,600 to 8,400 in Tableau 2022.1, then `MIN([Profit]) = -6,600`.

> **Note**
> There is a MIN function for many function types.

- ZN: ZN transforms `null` values into zero in a numerical field. This is helpful to see all data values/handling `null` values in Tableau. It will show all non-null values as they are—for example, `ZN(NULL) = 0` or `ZN(15) = 15`.

For a complete list of numerical functions, please review `https://help.tableau.com/current/pro/desktop/en-us/functions_functions_number.htm`.

String functions

String functions are used to manipulate text fields. Data may come in a little dirty when working with data visualization, so you may need to create splits, access a portion of data, or replace or trim it.

Tableau applies the **International Components for Unicode (ICU)** to compare strings—it uses the most up-to-date library, which can impact visualizations. For more information on that, please review the ICU website: `https://icu.unicode.org/home`. Here is a compiled list of basic string functions:

- LEFT: Used to pull the beginning or left part of a text value. It's useful when you know that an important value is contained within a specified number of characters at the beginning of a value—for example, `LEFT("Tableau",3) = Tab`.

> **Note**
> Blank spaces are included too as part of the character count.

- RIGHT: Used to pull the end or right part of a text value. It's useful when you know that an important value is contained within a specified number of characters at the end of a value—for example, `RIGHT("Salesforce",5) = force`.

> **Note**
> Blank spaces are included too as part of the character count.

- SPLIT: Adds text before or after a character search. A common one is to create new fields based on a specific value. A good example would be to extract only a first or last name from a name field. To pull the data after or before the character designation, start with (2) for after or (-2) for before. Here are three examples: `SPLIT("Jane Doe Johnson"," ",2) = "Doe"`, `SPLIT("Jane Doe Johnson",3) = "Johnson"`, and `SPLIT("Jane Doe Johnson,-3) = "Jane"`.

- TRIM: Removes blank text before and after the string. This is very important when data comes through with gaps. It will not clean up spaces between strings of text. Here are examples of each: `TRIM("  Jane Doe  ") = "Jane Doe"`, `LTRIM("  Jane Doe  ") = "Jane Doe  "`, and `RTRIM("  Jane Doe  ") = "  Jane Doe"`.

> **Note**
>
> `LTRIM` is similar but only focuses on the left side of the text, and `RTRIM` focuses only on the right side of the text.

For a complete list of string functions, please review `https://help.tableau.com/current/pro/desktop/en-us/functions_functions_string.htm`.

Date functions

Dates have a variety of uses in calculations, defining ranges, and grouping. Tableau offers a host of date functions to provide a wide range of additional capabilities to handle dates. The following is a list of common date functions:

- `DATEDIFF`: Creates a count of days between two date fields. You can also use a day of the week by name (for example, `'Monday'`, `'Tuesday'`, and so on) to further restrict, but this is less common. In this example, the order date is `6/20/22` `(MM/DD/YY)` and the ship date is `7/25/22`: `DATEDIFF('day',[Order Date],[Ship Date])=35` and `DATEDIFF('month',[Order Date],[Ship Date])=1`.

- `DATETRUNC`: Pulls a new date based on the criteria set for a date field. It's helpful for calculations or when you want to create date groups. You can also use a day of the week by name (for example, `'Monday'`, `'Tuesday'`, and so on) to further restrict, but this is less common. In these two examples, we are using an order from `6/30/21` `(MM/DD/YY)`: `DATETRUNC('year',"6/30/21")=1/1/21` `12:00:00` `AM` and `DATETRUNC('month",06/30/21")=6/1/21` `12:00:00 AM`.

> **Note**
> This will create a date and time field.

- `MAX`: Provides the maximum date from a date field. For example, order dates from the 2022.1 version of Tableau Public range from `1/3/18` `(MM/DD/YY)` to `12/30/21` `(MM/DD/YY)` then `MAX([Order Date]=12/30/21`.

- `MIN`: Provides the minimum date from a date field. For example, order dates from the 2022.1 version of Tableau Public range from `1/3/18` `(MM/DD/YY)` to `12/30/21` `(MM/DD/YY)`, then `MIN([Order Date]=1/3/18`.

- `TODAY`: Pulls the current date, which is helpful for calculations such as `DATEDIFF`. For example, if I am writing this on `7/31/22` `(MM/DD/YY)`, then `TODAY()=7/31/22`.

For a complete list of date functions, please review: `https://help.tableau.com/current/pro/desktop/en-us/functions_functions_date.htm`.

Logical functions

Logical functions are used when you want to create a conditional `true/false` statement. The following is a list of common logical functions:

- AND: The `AND` expression is a conditional statement that can be pulled from a dimension or measure that will yield a result—for example, `IF [Name]="John" AND [City Population]>5000 THEN "Urban John"`.

- CASE: A `CASE` statement is like an `IF` statement but simpler. However, it cannot apply many logical calculations due to only being able to assign a specific value when `'TRUE'` and additional clauses such as `AND` or `OR` cannot be used—for example, `CASE [State] WHEN "Wisconsin" THEN 1 WHEN "California" THEN 2 ELSE 0 END`.

- ELSE: `ELSE` provides an end value based on a test (commonly used with `CASE` and `IF` statements). `ELSE` is always used at the end of a nested or simple `IF` statement—for example, `IF COUNT([Orders])>100 THEN "Many Orders" ELSE "Few Orders" END`.

- ELSEIF: Use `ELSEIF` for nested `IF` statements when there are multiple conditions to a test—for example, `IF COUNT([Orders])>100 THEN "Many Orders" ELSEIF COUNT([Orders])>50 THEN "Moderate Orders" ELSE "Few Orders" END`.

> **Note**
> The last `ELSE` statement cannot be an `ELSEIF` statement; it must be `ELSE`.

- END: `END` closes the calculation for all calculations that test expressions. `END` is commonly used to end all calculations. For examples, see `CASE`, `ELSE`, and `ELSEIF`.

- IF: Used to test a series of expressions. An `IF` test can have one test or multiple/nested tests (with `ELSEIF`). For examples, see `ELSE` and `ELSEIF`.

- IFNULL: Used to provide a not null value if a field would otherwise return null—for example, `IFNULL([Order ID],"No Order")`. If the result is null, it will return `No Order`.

- IIF: Reviews a condition to see whether it's met. The met and unmet results need to be defined—for example, `IIF([CITY]="New York City", "Big Apple", "Not Big Apple")`. All cities that aren't `New York City` will be `"Not Big Apple"`.

- ISNULL: This is a `true/false` field that defines whether the result is null—for example, `ISNULL([Sales])`. If there was a null sale, then it would be `true`; otherwise, it would be `false`.

- MAX: For an explanation and examples, please see the preceding number, string, and date functions.

- MIN: For an explanation and examples, please see the preceding number, string, and date functions.

- OR: An expression is a conditional statement that can be pulled from a dimension or measure that will yield a result. For example, `IF [Customer Name]="John" OR [Customer Name]="Johnny" THEN "John" ELSE "Not John" END`. This will provide two results: `"John"` and `"Not John"`.

- THEN: Provides a result of a test on many logical tests or expressions. For examples, see AND, CASE, ELSE, and ELSEIF.

For a complete list of logical functions, please review `https://help.tableau.com/current/pro/desktop/en-us/functions_functions_logical.htm`.

Basic aggregate functions

Tableau works best with disaggregated data and provides many ways to aggregate data. The following is a list of common aggregate functions:

- AVG: Provides an average of values from a numeric field where null values aren't considered in the calculation—for example, `AVG(1,99,20)=40`.

- COUNT: Counts the number of non-null values from a group. For example, `COUNT([Order ID])` will count all order IDs in context.

> **Note**
> COUNT will count duplicates It is helpful for counting the total number of rows involved in a calculation.

- COUNTD: COUNTD counts distinct non-null values in a group. This is helpful if you want to use a count of the field as its lowest level of aggregation. For example, `COUNTD([Order ID])` will count the number of unique order IDs.

- MAX: For an explanation and examples, please see the preceding number, string, and date functions.

- MIN: For an explanation and examples, please see the preceding number, string, and date functions.

- SUM: Provides a total of values from a numeric field where null values aren't considered in the calculation—for example, `SUM(1,99,20)=120`.

For a complete list of aggregate functions, please review `https://help.tableau.com/current/pro/desktop/en-us/calculations_calculatedfields_aggregate_create.htm`.

Other functions

There are many other functions that can be used with Tableau, but they are less common, more complex, and not likely to be covered in the exam. Please review this Tableau help page if you want to review all available functions: `https://help.tableau.com/current/pro/desktop/en-us/functions.htm`.

As shared earlier, Tableau contains many functions. The functions highlighted in the previous sections are the ones you need to understand for the exam, but navigating through the lists will show you the power Tableau has with its extensive list and nearly infinite number of possibilities. In showing these functions, we also provided you with examples of calculations. Further, you will be able to build calculations on your own in the next section.

Creating basic calculations in Tableau

With data, you can often build visualizations with basic measures and dimensions. To add context, insight, and further clean the data, calculations are needed. For the examination, you do not need to be a calculations master, but you need to understand what basic calculations are and what they represent. This is what we will look at in the following subsections.

Creating a (blank) calculated field

You should select the down arrow shown in *Figure 5.1* and then click on **Create Calculated Field...** to start building a calculation:

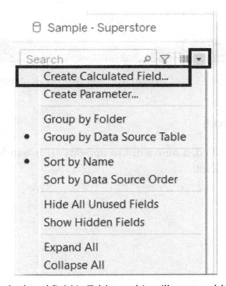

Figure 5.1 – Creating a calculated field in Tableau: this will create a blank calculation template

> **Tip**
>
> If you know which field you want to base a calculation on, then right-click on that field and select **Create | Calculated Field...** to get the field to show up immediately in the calculation. See *Figure 5.2* for an example.

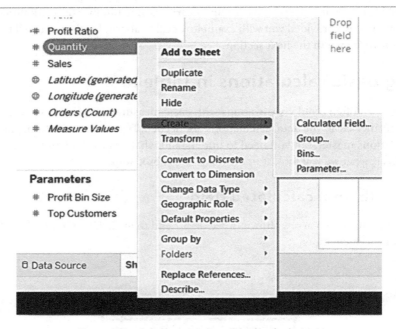

Figure 5.2 – Calculation editor (blank calculation)

Building a calculation

When a calculation field is called, a new window appears. This window is a calculation editor, as shown in the following screenshot:

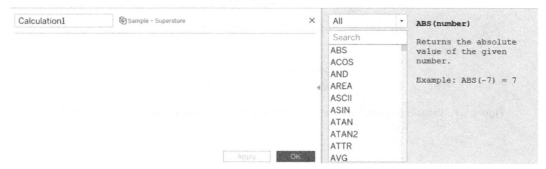

Figure 5.3 – Calculation editor (blank calculation)

> **Tip**
>
> If you do not see the help window when the editor is opened, there is a small arrow to the right of the editor that can be selected. I advise always keeping that section open to use it as a guide.

Next, I want to change the name of the calculated field to `Distinct Orders` by selecting the editable section where it shows `Calculation1` and typing `Distinct Orders` over it. I know I need to use the `COUNTD` function to count distinct orders. I also want to verify what `COUNTD` does, so I have the help dialog open on the right. *Figure 5.4* demonstrates what it shows. In addition, it shows that the calculation is not yet right as there is an error message at the bottom:

Figure 5.4 – Calculation part 2 (changing name, adding function, and using the help screen)

If I select **The calculation contains errors,** as shown in the preceding screenshot, it tells me that `COUNTD` is being called with `()` and asks whether I meant to use a Boolean. Although that is not a perfect error message, I know by looking at the help section that I need a field to call on it. Since we previously determined that `Order ID` is the field that provides the number of orders, let's see what happens when I include that field (see *Figure 5.5*):

Figure 5.5 – Completed (simple) calculation

With the field added, the statement at the bottom of the screen lets you know the calculation is added. This calculation will be a new field in your data. Any guess what type of field this will be? See *Figure 5.6* for the answer:

Figure 5.6 – Distinct Orders calculated field

Now, distinct orders show up as a calculation. Since we are counting, the field shows as a numeric field. Using the calculation and adding it as a text mark to the Distinct Orders sheet, we can see that the dataset includes 5,009 distinct orders. This calculation was not available until it was created using the calculation editor.

Calculations can be utilized using all the previous function examples. Remember—many functions have rules. If you reach an error, please leave your help dialog open and search for the function. Also, for the exam, most questions about calculations will be relatively simple. Relevant questions related to calculations have been added to the *Knowledge check* section.

Next, we need to cover just a brief introduction to LOD expressions and parameters.

Introduction to LOD expressions and parameters

LOD expressions and parameters are some of the most powerful yet least understood elements for newer Tableau users. We will go a little deeper into these concepts in future chapters but want to make sure you are introduced to the very basics in this section.

LOD expressions

LOD expressions show up as standard calculations and can be included as part of a standard calculation. The purpose of LOD calculations is to create a measurement at a defined level of aggregation. When creating most calculations, the LOD is dependent on what is in the workbook, defined details, or filters. There are three LOD calculations (Fixed, Include, and Exclude) to help independently define the details seen on the visualization that we will look at in the following list. Please review the *Order of operations* section to see how filters and other pieces impact your visualization.

- **Fixed**—This is a LOD expression that looks at the referenced dimension or dimensions to determine what a value should be. LOD expressions are defined by {}, where regular calculations and functions are surrounded by (). The format of a fixed LOD is {Dimension1, Dimension2: Aggregated Measure}. For example, in our superstore data, we can use Order ID and Sales to get sales by order ID. Fixed is the most common LOD used and would be the likely question for LOD expressions in the exam. *Figure 5.7* includes an example of a LOD in practice:

Figure 5.7 – LOD (Fixed) example

In this example, I wanted to find, without using other dimensions, the average value of a sale for an order in my dataset. I did not want to create any filters or anything; just answer a question that couldn't be otherwise answered. I wanted to get the average of each sale, so I used AVG based on my order ID. Note that I also modified my mark to AVG (instead of SUM) to match the intended data output.

- **Include**: This is a LOD that includes values only based on the dimension or dimensions selected.

- **Exclude**: This specifies which values to exclude from the view based on the selected dimensions.

Although Include and Exclude have use cases, they are less common and not likely to be asked in the examination. Regardless, Tableau does provide detailed information on LOD expressions, including example calculations, in their help section: https://help.tableau.com/current/pro/desktop/en-us/calculations_calculatedfields_lod.htm.

Parameters

Parameters are workbook variables that require another entity (usually a calculation) to empower the variable. Parameters are user generated and can take the form of float, integer, string, Boolean, date, or date and time. Parameters can be fixed or dynamic depending on how they are used, but *ALWAYS* require a helper. Unlike calculations, they can be enacted on a worksheet level but can be used, if empowered, on an entire workbook.

Parameters are superheroes that need a helper. For a superhero analogy, think of parameters as Batman and calculations as Robin.

Since parameters are somewhat an intermediate topic, this exam will not go into too much detail—besides the basics—on parameters. However, understanding parameters will provide an opportunity to extend the capabilities of your Tableau work.

For more on parameters, please review this help article on Tableau: `https://help.tableau.com/current/pro/desktop/en-us/parameters_create.htm`.

LOD expressions and parameters provide more capabilities than what standard calculations can offer. Although a deep understanding of them isn't required for the specialist examination, understanding them will help enhance your Tableau knowledge as well as empower stronger data visualization capabilities. To better understand how Tableau interacts with calculations, dimensions, and LOD expressions, the order of operations in Tableau needs an introduction.

Order of operations

As with many functional entities, Tableau also has an **order of operations**. It is the key to understanding how your visualization will respond to various influences.

Tableau's order of operations is visualized and explained by Tableau in detail in this help section: `https://help.tableau.com/current/pro/desktop/en-us/order_of_operations.htm`.

Tableau does an incredible job of providing its explanation, but to provide its impact on your examination, we will share key takeaways for the examination, as follows:

- Adding filters in context is more powerful than any set, group, calculation, or LOD expression

> **Note**
> Since parameters depend on one of these filters, context filters (or the most powerful worksheet filter) will neutralize any parameter. Please review `https://help.tableau.com/current/pro/desktop/en-us/order_of_operations.htm` to refresh your memory on how to create a filter in context.

- Fixed LOD expressions are the most powerful LOD expression, whereas Include/Exclude are the least powerful

- Dimension filters are more powerful than measure filters but less powerful than LOD expressions

- Table calculations are the least powerful calculations but supersede trend and reference lines, which are at the bottom of Tableau's order of operation

As previously iterated, knowing Tableau's order of operations is key to understanding how various actions impact a visualization in Tableau. Please review the help section (linked in the preceding information box) to further extend your knowledge of this important concept.

Summary

In this chapter, you learned how to utilize Tableau's large set of functions and how to build a calculation and check its functionality, and saw how LOD expressions and parameter functions work within the rules of Tableau's order of operations. Understanding these concepts elevates your capabilities with the tool and significantly helps you to master the *Tableau Desktop Specialist* certification.

In the next chapter, we will further support your data work as we explore connecting and preparing data on Tableau Desktop.

Knowledge check

To check your knowledge of this chapter, here are a few questions that this chapter's material will help you answer. The questions that have been selected aren't intended to trick you but to provide you with a learning benchmark to give you a foundational understanding to help prepare you for the exam. The answers are marked in italics:

1. The TRIM function provides the combined capabilities of the LTRIM and RTRIM functions.

    A. True

    B. *False*

2. How can you verify the validity of a calculation in the calculation editor?

    A. Tableau understands your entries in calculation and will automate a calculation if one cannot be found.

    B. *There is an indicator at the bottom of the calculation editor that informs a user whether a calculation is valid.*

    C. There is no way to test a calculation unless it is added to a visualization.

3. According to Tableau's order of operations, which LOD calculation is the most powerful?

    A. Parameters

    B. Excluded

    C. *Fixed*

    D. Include

    E. None of these

4. What would this formula yield: ABS (-200)?

    A. 0

    B. -200

    C. *200*

    D. None of these

5. See the following image and please select why the calculation created an error.

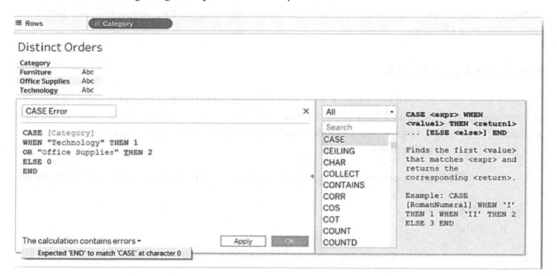

Figure 5.8 – Calculation window with the help section exposed

    A. The calculation was incomplete.

    B. There is no instance of Technology or Office Supplies under Category.

    C. The CASE statement resulted in a value instead of a string.

    D. *"OR" was used in a CASE function.*

Part 2: Mastering the Exam

In *Part 2*, we will build on the core basics of *Part 1* to extend your understanding of the Tableau fundamentals. This section is truly a blend of approaches to most efficiently expedite your knowledge of and capabilities with Tableau.

The second part contains four chapters, starting with more advanced data applications on the desktop, then creating actual charts with detailed instructions, applying additional analytics and organizing data, creating a dashboard, and applying analytics and actions at the worksheet and dashboard level.

By the end of this part, you will have all the knowledge needed to master the Tableau Desktop Certification examination, especially if you utilize the exercises to reinforce your ability to use the tool practically.

This part comprises the following chapters:

- *Chapter 6, Connecting to and Preparing Data*
- *Chapter 7, Understanding and Creating Fundamental Charts in Tableau*
- *Chapter 8, Data Organization and Worksheet Analytics*
- *Chapter 9, Sharing Insights*

6

Connecting to and Preparing Data

To develop a visualization, you need to have data to work with. Tableau Desktop accepts many data sources, including text, Excel, many types of databases, and Tableau-hosted data sources, to name a few, and offers a range of basic functions. This enables you to have a lot of data flexibility and not have to use a separate ETL tool in many instances to prepare data for your requirements.

In this chapter, you will learn when and how to apply live or extracted data, how to create live data connections and extracts, and how to store those data connections. Then, you will learn how to create joins, unions, and relationships in Tableau and how to apply them. Finally, you will grasp how to change a field name, add an alias, assign geography, and manage data types and properties.

In this chapter, we will cover the following topics:

- Creating live data connections and extracts
- Creating and managing the Tableau data model
- Managing data properties

Technical requirements

In this chapter, you will need the following to apply hands-on learning:

- A Tableau Desktop application: Most versions will work with the exam, but for best results, use 2021.1 or later. The location of the current download is `https://www.tableau.com/products/desktop/download`. This version is not free but allows for a 2-week trial. In earlier chapters, the Tableau Public Application would work, but not in this case.

> **Note**
> The Tableau Public Application will not be useful for learning about these concepts, as data stored on Tableau Public is automatically extracted.

- The *Superstore Sales* dataset: This automatically comes with the Tableau Desktop application but can also be pulled into the Tableau Public application by downloading it from Tableau Resources here: `https://public.tableau.com/en-us/s/resources?qt-overview_resources=1#qt-overview_resources`.

- Excel or Google Sheets to create a new data source: Instructions on what to add to the data source will be included. The example will be using Excel but can be replicated in Google Sheets.

Creating live data connections and extracts

We covered some data connection basics beginning in *Chapter 2*. In Tableau, data can be connected live or extracted. Before learning how to create these connections, it's important to learn the benefits of each of them based on the separate features you look for when working with data connections.

Live versus extracted connections

Data can be connected live or static (or extracted). There are many considerations you need to consider with these connection types and how it impacts your needs and the performance of the workbooks. The following section will cover the major aspects of live versus extracted connections.

Data recency

Live connections mean the data flows into Tableau Desktop as soon as the source data is updated. With extracts, the extract needs to be refreshed to show updated data. The data freshness is fully dependent on when it was last updated or refreshed.

When the freshness of the data is vital, a live connection is often the better option. When data is static or only needs to be refreshed ad hoc, an extract often works best.

> **Important note**
> A "live" connection may be a misnomer in many situations. For example, data can flow into a data warehouse in real time, but a table in between may only be updated at certain intervals. As a result, the data may not be live, but will be updated as soon as that table is refreshed.

Performance/speed

Extracted connections work much quicker than live after the initial extraction. Tableau embeds the data in the workbook, which reduces load times as it does not need to call data from an outside source.

> **Note**
>
> The impact of speed is greater when there is more data involved. For example, if the data table is small, then you may not notice any change in speed. However, if the data comes from millions of records and uses many filters and sheets, then the difference in speed/performance is significant. Also, live connections with many records can take a long time to refresh.

Offline work

Live connections require an internet connection; therefore, an offline user cannot use live connections – users must be connected to the internet. Extracts, on the other hand, can be used without being dependent on any connection outside of working with the Desktop application.

> **Note**
>
> If using the Tableau Public application, which strongly resembles the Desktop application in functionality, a workbook cannot be saved without being connected to your Tableau Public account and requires an internet connection – however, if the data is extracted, the workbook can be worked on.

There are more considerations when using extracts versus live connections, but the three we have covered are the main considerations when working with Desktop and not considering Tableau Server or Cloud data sources.

For more information about extracted data from Tableau, please visit this *help* article: `https://help.tableau.com/current/pro/desktop/en-us/extracting_data.htm`.

Creating a live data connection

We covered the basics of data ingestion in *Chapter 2*. With Tableau Desktop, you can create live data sources or extract the data source. Tableau defaults to live connections when connecting with data for the first time, but if you create a packaged workbook, it will require the data to be extracted.

We are now going to see how to create a live connection. To create a live data connection, simply open your Desktop and pull a file or a database as this is the default starting point when opening your Desktop. Select **Connect to Data**. In this example, you can pull the **Sample – Superstore** dataset. This is an Excel file:

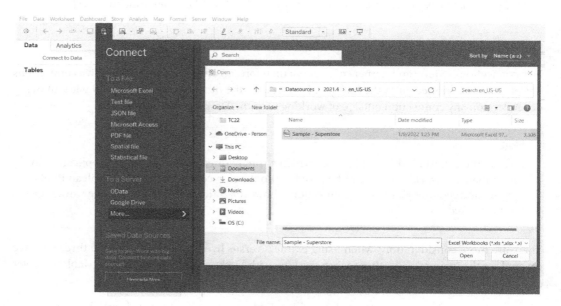

Figure 6.1: Connecting to a live data source on Tableau Desktop

> **Tip**
>
> You can use any Excel file to follow along but downloading the **Sample – Superstore** dataset from the Desktop application will go into your Tableau Data Repository in datasets so you have more immediate access to the data as needed.

Once connected, all tables will appear on the left side of the **Sheets** section.

As shown in the following screenshot, Tableau instructs you where to drag tables to be able to use the data:

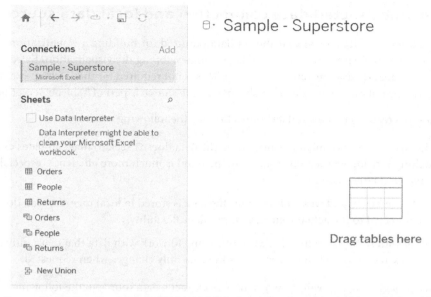

Figure 6.2: Tableau Desktop (Public) initial data ingestion from Excel with multiple tables

Next up, drag the **Orders** named range from the **Sheets** section to the **Drag tables here** location. This process will let Tableau know you have data to work with. In the following screenshot, we can see what this process looks like and how Tableau Desktop automatically marks the connection as **Live**:

Figure 6.3: Dragging Orders to the data pane with the default "Live" connection

At this point, you can go to a worksheet to begin working with the data or add more tables to the mix. However, we will stop here as we have already made a live data connection. Next up, I want to create a time-stamped or extract of the dataset, as I want total control of when the data is updated.

Creating an extracted data connection and local data source

A Tableau extract supplies a local snapshot of data required for building a visualization. It stores the extracted data, so the information has no lag when developing the visualization. Extracts can be refreshed per manual request on Tableau Desktop. This is not required for the Desktop examination, but extracts can be put on a scheduled refresh when a data source is part of Tableau Server or Cloud.

You will want to create an extracted data connection for the following reasons:

- Workbook and development performance: The data doesn't seek to make updates every time something is being worked on in Tableau; the build is much more efficient – especially when working with large datasets.

- The data can be worked with offline: Since the data is stored in local memory, you do not need to be connected to the actual source, so it provides flexibility.

- Working with stable data: It can be very confusing to work with data that constantly changes. With an extract, you have total control, as the data only changes when requested.

Creating an extract is simple. I will show you how to extract a data source in the following two ways:

- Creating an extract from the **Data Source** tab
- Creating an extract from a sheet

Let's dive in!

Creating an extract from the Data Source tab

The following are the instructions to create an extract quickly:

1. From the **Data Source** pane, toggle the radio button from **Live** to **Extract** in the **Connection** section, which you will find in the upper-right corner of the screen (note that it will not try to extract until you leave the tab or request to save the file):

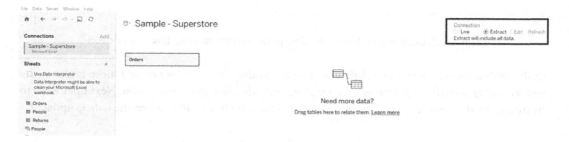

Figure 6.4: Selecting Extract in the data pane

2. Go to **Sheet 1** from the **Data Source** pane, which is the first default sheet in a Tableau workbook, as shown in the following screenshot:

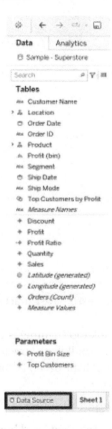

Figure 6.5: Going to the (default) Sheet 1 from the Data Source tab

3. A dialog will pop up automatically, as shown in *Figure 6.6*. Set **File name** to My Sample Extract. Select **Save**:

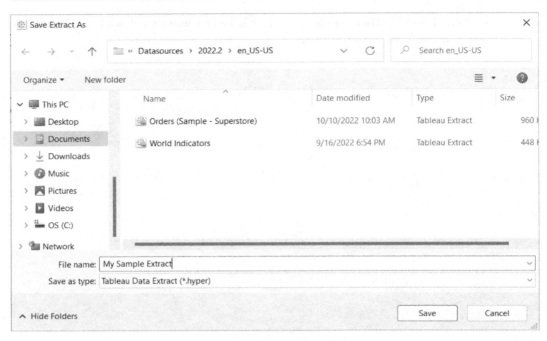

Figure 6.6: Save Extract As

4. You will want to save the workbook too (naming is covered in the next step). It will need to be saved as a packaged workbook to pull that extracted file named My Sample Extract. This will also help you easily locate that extract. From **Sheet 1**, select **File | Save As**. A dialog box will appear, as shown in *Figure 6.7*.

5. Change **File name** to My Packaged Workbook.

6. From **Save as type**, select **Tableau Packaged Workbook** (it will default to **Tableau Workbook**, but you will need to select packaged workbook, which is option 2). Now, your dialog box should resemble *Figure 6.7*:

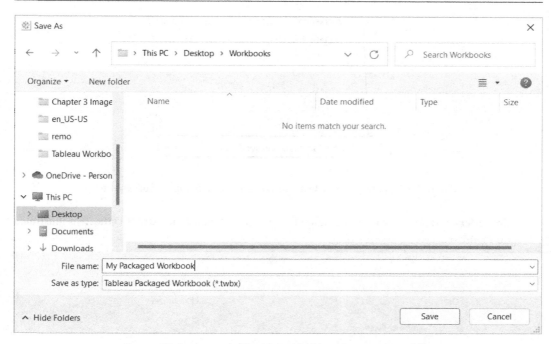

Figure 6.7: Saving a packaged workbook with an extracted file

At this point, the workbook can be closed, and you can call on it with the extracted data source at any point.

Creating an extract from a sheet

Here are the steps to create an extracted data source from a sheet. You may want to do this if you have multiple data sources or need more immediate access to the **Extract Data** dialog box shown in *Figure 6.10*:

1. From the **Data Source** pane, go to **Sheet 1**.

2. Then, go to **Data | Orders (Sample - Superstore)**, as shown in the following screenshot:

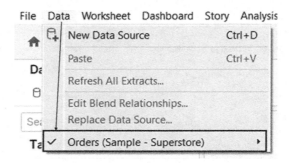

Figure 6.8: Selecting the Orders named range from Sample - Superstore

3.   In **Orders**, select the arrow to the right of the name and then pick **Extract Data...**, as illustrated in *Figure 6.9*:

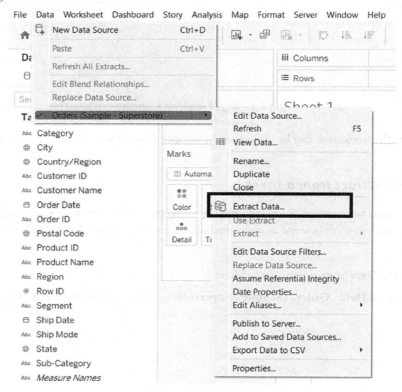

Figure 6.9: Accessing Extract Data from Orders

4.   Once you select **Extract Data**, a popup will appear. It should look like *Figure 6.10*. It defaults to the correct options, so select **Extract**:

Figure 6.10: Extract Data dialog box

5. To verify whether an extract has been created, go back to the **Data Source** tab and verify that the **Connection** section (as seen in *Figure 6.11*) is set to **Extract** rather than **Live**:

Figure 6.11: Extracted data source verification

6. You will want to save the workbook too (the workbook name will be covered in the next step). It will need to be saved as a packaged workbook to pull that extracted file. This will also help you easily locate that extract. From **Sheet 1**, select **File | Save As**. A dialog box will appear, as shown in *Figure 6.12*.

7. Rename the file to My Packaged Workbook 2.

8. From **Save as type**, select **Tableau Packaged Workbook** (it will default to **Tableau Workbook**, but you will need to select the packaged workbook, which is option 2). Now, your dialog box should resemble *Figure 6.12*:

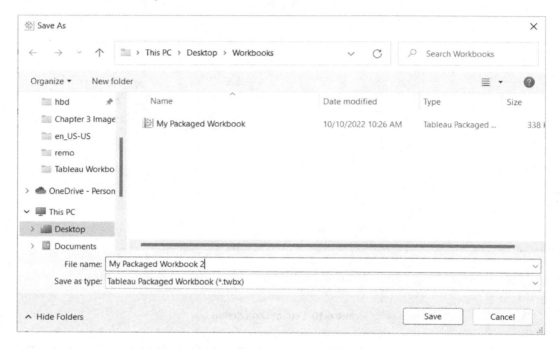

Figure 6.12: Saving a packaged workbook with an extracted file

At this point, the workbook can be closed, and you can call on it with the extracted data source at any point.

Notes

You will not need to deep-dive into all the **Save** options that Tableau provides for the Tableau Desktop Certification. But briefly, Tableau defaults to logical tables, and extract filters can be added to limit the availability of data coming in, can make data aggregates at the source level, can restrict the number of rows coming in, and can even hide all unused rows.

For more information on these items, please review Tableau's article, here: `https://help.tableau.com/current/pro/desktop/en-us/extracting_data.htm#create-an-extract`.

In this section, we further learned about the difference between live and extracted data, and we created live and extracted data sources. Next, we need to cover Tableau's data model; we often need to work with multiple data sources and relate them somehow. Tableau has its own version of a data model, and you will learn about it and the basics of its application next.

Creating and managing the data model

Your Tableau Desktop Specialist Certification exam will have some questions covering the data model, but don't worry. You do not need to be a SQL expert or have a super fine-grained understanding of this part. For this section, we will cover the necessary literacy and knowledge to answer the exam questions confidently and accurately. In the following subsections, we will cover what needs to be understood regarding Tableau's relationship model.

What is Tableau's data model?

The data model in Tableau is Tableau's way of creating relationships on Tableau Desktop. It is like SQL where it's effectively a join, but more powerful, as it can determine the data's best fit to apply a relationship as it seeks the best way to join and blend the data based on its given parameters. Each table shows up as its own entity when working with the data but also works fluently, as the relationship is defined well. Tableau calls these inter-table relationships joins **noodles**. *Figure 6.13* shows these noodles from **Orders** to **People** and **Returns**:

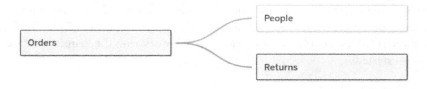

Figure 6.13: Tableau data model (relationships) using the Sample - Superstore dataset

Tableau tries to find a common link between the data sources. Hence, in this example, clicking on either of these noodles tells you where the link is between the two data sources. As shown in *Figure 6.14*, **Orders** and **Returns** are linked by **Order ID**. However, you can create your own link or multiple links by changing the join option or selecting the plus sign beneath the **Order ID** join, as shown in *Figure 6.14*:

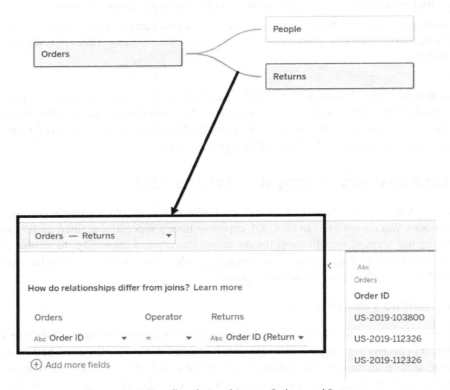

Figure 6.14: Noodle relationships on Orders and Returns

Creating a simple data model

In the preceding section, we saw a model in action. However, to further understand the Tableau data model, we need to create our own relationship. Not to worry, Tableau makes it very simple to create relationships. To get started, you will need to access your Superstore Excel dataset. It should have three sheets: **Orders**, **People**, and **Returns**. You will work with the **People** and **Orders** named ranges. Let's get started!

1.   Open Tableau Desktop.

2.   Connect to **Data** (which is covered in *Figure 6.1*) and select **Sample - Superstore**.

3.   Drag the **Orders** (named range) to the **Drag tables here** section.

4. Pull the **People** named range to the right of **Orders**. Did you notice how the noodle follows **People** when you drag it over? Now, release the **People** table. Once done, it should look like *Figure 6.15*:

Figure 6.15: Basic relationship in Tableau Desktop or one-to-one logical table relationship

Check out *Figure 6.16* to see the details about the relationship and fields. You can see that the table is connected via two common fields (**Region**). You did not need to identify the relationship, as Tableau could detect it automatically.

> **Note**
>
> If Tableau cannot determine the relationship, the noodle will have a dotted line and an exclamation mark to alert you to define the field or fields in each table to create the relationship, as covered in *Figure 6.14*.

Figure 6.16: Orders and People relationship details

> **Note**
>
> Relationships can be made with multiple file types by adding a connection.

In this section, you understood Tableau's native and flexible approach to modeling and were able to develop a data relationship yourself. The next section covers more about data properties. We will continue working with our dataset to cover some aspects of this approach.

Managing data properties

Data does not always come in clean. In this section, we will go into more detail about manipulating data fields. Tableau does an excellent job of assigning field types, but there are times when it makes sense to update fields. Besides that, data does not always come in with good field names or needs aliases to work with your visualization. In this section, we will cover the necessary data properties that haven't already been covered in other places throughout this book, such as changing default properties and reviewing data properties that can be changed.

In the following exercise, we will first look at **Ship Date**. The real **Ship Date** field comes in as a Date field, but I changed the Date field to String to provide an example of the data properties.

> **Note**
>
> To try this exercise yourself, you will be able to execute this exercise based on the following example (except that you will have to change **Ship Date** to String and then back to Date).

Our first example is the **Ship Date** field that came into Tableau as a string, but you know it's a Date field. As you can see in *Figure 6.17*, the **Ship Date** field appears as a string because, on the left, it has the **Abc** icon rather than a calendar icon:

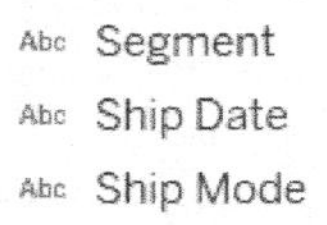

Abc Segment

Abc Ship Date

Abc Ship Mode

Figure 6.17: Ship Date

Now, you want to make sure the field is a Date field. So, how do you change it?

To change, simply right-click on the field name, select **Change Data Type**, and select **Date** instead of **String**:

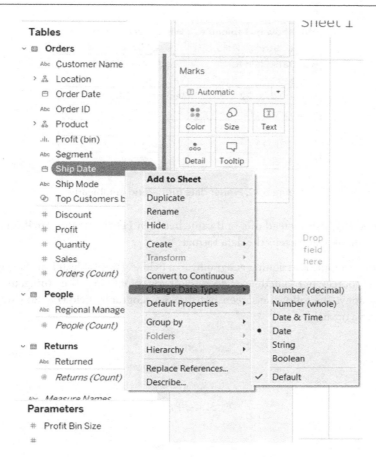

Figure 6.18: Accessing Change Data Type options

As seen in *Figure 6.18*, you can do this to flip data types between **String**, **Date** (standard `Date` field), **Date & Time** (a `Date` field with a timestamp in HH:MM format by default), **Number (whole)** or **Number (decimal)**, and **Default** (or what Tableau picks).

Now, this is important to note. Tableau is good at picking the correct data types on most occasions. In many instances, like when Tableau reads a field as a string instead of a date, it's because there is another non-date and non-null value that is part of the field, and a field needs to be all or nothing to be defined as something that's not a string (a `String` field is a catch-all).

For example, a common error is when a `Date` field includes a date and `N/A` in some rows where there aren't dates. Since `N/A` cannot be interpreted as a date, the field may error if trying to change from a string to a date without cleaning up the `N/A` in the data source. See the example in *Figure 6.19*:

Will show in Tableau as a "String" Field	Will show in Tableau as a "Date" Field
Bad Date Field for Tableau	Good Date Field for Tableau
January 1, 2022	January 1, 2022
February 1, 2022	February 1, 2022
N/A	
April 1, 2022	April 1, 2022
May 1, 2022	May 1, 2022

Figure 6.19: Proper date formatting in Tableau

Please notice where N/A is instead of a null value between **February** and **April** on the right-hand side. That null or blank value keeps the data format.

Another common example is assigning geography to a field. Again, Tableau is usually good at finding geography in data sources, but sometimes it does not. If you want to map something, then it's important to find the geography. The following screenshot shows a geography field (**Postal Code**) showing up as a standard String field:

∨ ⛬ Location
    ⊕ Country/Region
    ⊕ Region
    ⊕ State/Province
    ⊕ City
    Abc Postal Code

Figure 6.20: Postal Code showing up without geography

In *Figure 6.20*, we can see that **Postal Code** does not have the geography icon but instead has a string icon (**Abc**). Although Tableau can map the **Postal Code** field as a dimension, it ignores the geographical part. Surely we want to make sure geographic fields show up as such.

Similar to the prior example, we just need to right-click the field, but select **Geographic Role** instead of **Change Data Type**. Sure enough, in *Figure 6.21*, we can see that **None** was selected:

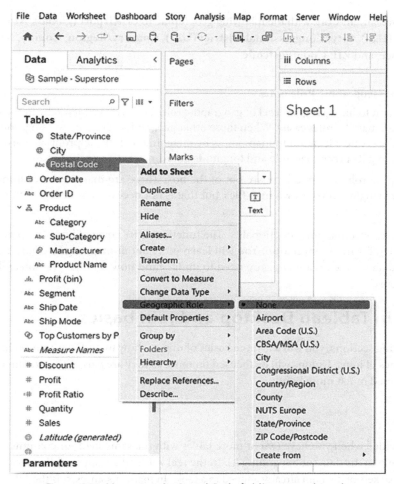

Figure 6.21: Managing the Postal Code field's geographic role

To map to the proper geographic role, simply select **ZIP Code/Postcode** from the list and the geographic property will align.

As shown, Tableau can work with the following geographic roles: **Airport (global)**, **Area Code (U.S.)**, **CBSA/MSA (U.S.)**, **City**, **Congressional District (U.S.)**, **Country/Region**, **County**, **NUTS Europe**, **State/Province**, and **ZIP Code/Postcode**.

Important Geographic Role notes

It's important to have a higher level of geographic roles and create a hierarchy in the dataset so Tableau can map the roles easily. When those other geographic levels are missing, you will need to manually create a location to map points by matching with the appropriate corresponding role or having its precise latitude and longitude coordinates.

The mapping roles covered here are out of the box. There are many more custom options, including bringing in your own map files, but that is not necessary to cover for this exam.

Tableau has a robust mapping functionality. The functionalities covered here are some of the basics that are needed for the examination. You will learn more about mapping in *Chapter 7*. To further understand data source organizing, you need to understand how unions function and have a brief tutorial on joins.

Unions in Tableau Desktop and join basics

In the following sections, you will learn the basics of unions, how to perform a union in Tableau, and learn the basics of joins. Unions will be focused on more as they are part of the examination, whereas joins are covered much more lightly.

Unions

Unions are added when you have two or more tables with the same fields or columns. All the user is doing is adding to the data (or appending it). In the real world, data can come in piecemeal, meaning that you get packets of data not already aligned to a table. In many instances, it is the Tableau developer's responsibility to structure it well for visualization. *Figure 6.22* will show how it works:

Table 1

Date	Sales State	Sales Amount
11/11/2022	California	$75.26
11/13/2022	Maryland	$15.45
11/16/2022	California	$300.25

Table 2

Date	Sales State	Sales Amount
10/15/2022	Wisconsin	$ 87.45
12/4/2002	Texas	$ 1,205.00
11/11/2022	Nevada	$ 478.96

Union Result (Table 1 + Table 2 in one combined table)

Date	Sales State	Sales Amount
44876	California	75.26
44878	Maryland	15.45
44881	California	300.25
44849	Wisconsin	87.45
37594	Texas	1205
44876	Nevada	478.96

Figure 6.22: Union configuration

Figure 6.22 shows that Table 1 and Table 2 have the same fields (Date, Sales State, and Sales Amount, with data in the same format. Although both tables contain three rows, the number of rows does not matter. What matters is that columns and their data structure are consistent. Knowing how unions work, let's see how this can be done in Tableau.

On Tableau Desktop, you will see how this can be accomplished. In fact, you will be creating your own union.

Instructions on how to create your first union

Perform the following steps to create your first union:

1. Create a spreadsheet with two sheets (one called `Table 1` and the other called `Table 2`) with the same names, data, and data structure, as shown in *Figure 6.22*.

2. Save the spreadsheet as `Union Example`.

3. Open Tableau Desktop and connect to that `Union Example` file.

4. When connected, it should look like *Figure 6.23*:

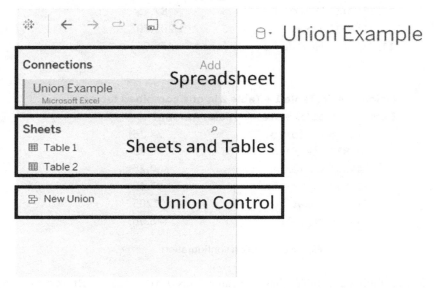

Figure 6.23: The Data Source tab with Union Example

5. Select **New Union,** as seen in **Union Control** in *Figure 6.23*.

6. Drag tables 1 and 2 from **Sheets** and select **OK**. Note that the sheets should look like *Figure 6.24*:

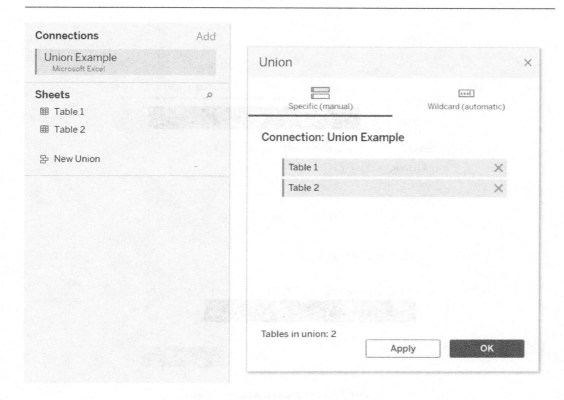

Figure 6.24: Union of Table 1 and Table 2

After you select **OK**, the union is made. You will notice a new column or field when storing that, called **Table Name**. This is stored metadata informing you which table or sheet it came from; in this example, they came from a sheet.

Wildcard (automatic) unions

Wildcard unions are more advanced. Here, you use a wildcard character or an asterisk (*) to designate a pattern for Desktop to pull from your data connection.

With our Table 1 and Table 2 example, if you entered *1 as seen in *Figure 6.25*, you will have a union with any table that comes into **Union Example** with a 1 or just Table 1 with the current example. However, if you get sheets with 1 in them, then they will automatically get unioned.

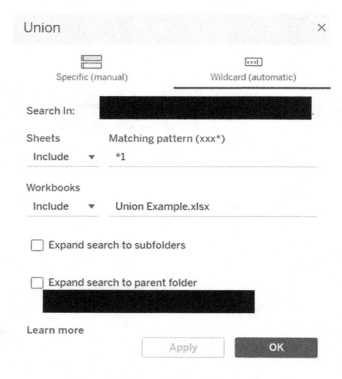

Figure 6.25: Example of a wildcard union

Tableau provides a lot more detail on unions at `https://help.tableau.com/current/pro/desktop/en-us/union.htm`, but you have the basics you need for the examination. However, I will add a couple of notes next.

Union considerations

Here are few things that needs to be considered while using unions:

- Unions can be edited once connected, so you can change from manual to wildcard or vice versa, manage wildcard considerations, or remove a union

- Mismatched fields when unioned results in null values for the table that doesn't share that field name – any change in field names between sheets or tables has a significant impact on unions

- Tableau defaults to using the first row on sheets if it detects it there, or will look for what appears to be a header or field name in your datasheet

- Another way to create a union on the **Data Source** pane is to drag a table on the **Drag tables here** pane and then another table can be dragged on top of the table on the pane; then select **Union**

Although unions will be more of an exam focus, the fundamentals of joins in Tableau need coverage too.

Join basics

Joins are not unions or relationships. Older versions of Tableau Desktop did not have a relationship model but defaulted to relationships. Tableau supports four join types: inner joins or only grabbing rows where the information matches both tables; full outer joins or a join that contains all data from each table where non-matching fields result in null values; and left or right joins or full data from one table (situated on the left or right side, respectively), and matching values from the other table.

Tableau still maintains a physical layer underneath the logical layer. This layer can contain joins and is accessible when double-clicking on any logical table. If the logical layer only includes one table, no joins would be seen. For even more on this, please see https://help.tableau.com/current/online/en-us/datasource_relationships_learnmorepage.htm.

Although joins still have some purpose on Tableau Desktop, they are very seldom used because of the power of relationships. In addition, there are niche times they can be used.

Summary

In this chapter, you learned about live and extracted data connections and how to connect them. You also learned about the basics of creating Tableau's data model, and how to manage data properties from the Tableau worksheet model. These elements are necessary for *Domain 1: Connecting to and Preparing data*, which is 25% of the test's score.

In the next chapter, you will get more hands-on by creating basic charts, organizing data, applying filters, and applying additional basic analytic analysis.

Knowledge check

1. How do you make a connection in Tableau Desktop live? (Check all that apply.)

    A. Create an extract

    B. *The default for connecting a new data source is a live connection once at least one table is brought in*

    C. *Deselect* **Use Extract** *from any worksheet*

    D. *Change the selection in the* **Data Source** *tab from* **Extract** *to* **Live** *under* **Connection**

2. What are the reasons you would want to work with a data extract? (Check all that apply.)

    A. *Speed/performance are typically improved*

    B. You get the most recent data from the initial data source

    C. *You can work with the data offline*

3. How does the Tableau relationship model work?

    A. A user creates left, center, right, or outer joins to connect tables in the logical layer defined by one or more common fields in each table

    B. You cannot add more than one data table to Tableau Desktop

    C. *Using a logical layer, noodles are joined between two or more tables defined by one or more common fields in each table*

    D. None of the above

4. Which is not an option in **Change Data Type**?

    A. *Geography*

    B. String

    C. Number

    D. Date

Understanding and Creating Fundamental Charts in Tableau

In this chapter, we'll begin to have real fun by creating charts from data. You will learn how to create 11 common charts in Tableau, about their applications, and how to recreate them with your data. This chapter will cover the knowledge required for 35% of the exam's scoring.

In this chapter, we will cover the following topics:

- Creating fundamental charts without using Ask Me
- Understanding use cases based on a chart insight exploration

Technical requirements

You will need the following for hands-on learning in this chapter:

- The Tableau Desktop application. Most versions will work for the exam, but for the best results, use 2021.1 or later. The location of current downloads can be found at `https://www. tableau.com/products/desktop/download`. This version is not free but you do get a 2-week trial.

- A version that has similar functionality to Tableau Desktop but that's free is Tableau Public. It does not have all the same data and extension functionality as the Tableau Desktop application but has everything you need for the Tableau Desktop Specialist certification. It is available here: `https://public.tableau.com/en-us/s/download`. If you've downloaded it already, please use version 2021.1 or later.

- The Superstore Sales dataset. It automatically comes with Tableau Desktop.

Creating fundamental charts

Tableau provides you with the flexibility to create a wide range of almost limitless charts, limited only by your creativity and advanced mathematics skills. Fortunately, the charts you will learn about for the Tableau Desktop Specialist Exam do not require you to implement trigonometry, geometry, or calculus. In my 10 years of professional experience with the tool, these charts cover well over 90% of use cases. In the next few sub-sections, we will learn how to create basic charts, maps, and multiple-axis charts.

In the following sections, we will cover the following basic charts, all of which will be covered in the exam:

- Bar chart
- Crosstab or data table
- Highlight table
- Stacked bar chart
- Line chart
- Area chart
- Scatter plot
- Dual-axis chart
- Filled map
- Point Map
- Density Map

Let us begin!

Bar chart

A **bar chart** is the most visual chart type, and one of the most easily understood. Bar charts are used to compare data or measures categorically. The standard bar chart shows the categories by rows. These rows can also be flipped to columns. A chart with columns would still be classed as a bar chart but is often referred to as a **column chart**.

Using our Sample-Superstore data source, we can see the sum of profits by region. To do that, put **Region** (a discrete dimension) on **Rows** and **Profit** (a continuous measure) on **Columns**, as seen in *Figure 7.1*:

Note

Since **Profit** is a continuous measure, the measure will default to **Sum** (or **SUM(Profit)**) unless we identify a different calculation.

Figure 7.1: Adding data to create a chart

When you do this, you will see we have made our first chart type. Since we have a measure on **Columns** and a dimension on **Rows**, Tableau will automatically generate a bar chart, as shown in *Figure 7.2*:

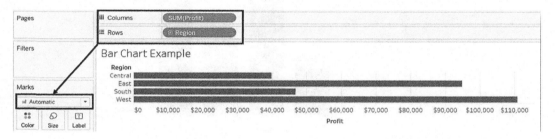

Figure 7.2: Tableau automatically creates a bar chart when a continuous measure is paired with a discrete dimension

As we can see, in the **Marks** section, the chart type that's displayed is **Automatic** but shows an icon of a bar chart– a column chart – to its left, signifying a bar chart is what is being shown.

Note

The bar chart symbol for this will always be the column chart.

With that, we have decided that we want to see it as a column chart or with the bars vertically rather than horizontally. There are two ways to quickly do this:

- We can manually move **Region** to **Columns** and **Profit** to **Rows**.
- We can select the **Swap Rows and Columns** icon above **Rows**, as seen in *Figure 7.3*:

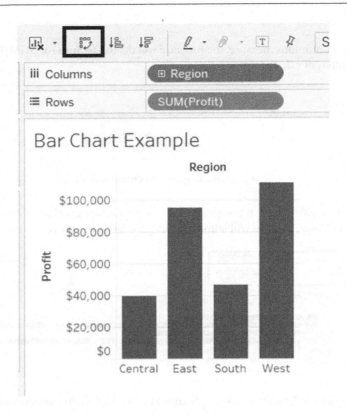

Figure 7.3: Swap Rows and Columns to flip the chart's orientation

If you created these charts with me, do not forget to save your progress for the next section.

Now that you know how to create bar charts in two ways, you will want to add a little context to illustrate more information about what the viewer is seeing. Tableau makes this remarkably simple, but you need to know how to get there to semi-automatically generate a crosstab or text table.

Crosstab (text table)

Even with a wonderful visual medium and a robust number of chart types available, most personas prefer to use tables as they are familiar. Hence, **crosstabs** or **text tables** are the next best thing offered by Tableau whenever you want to see the data as is and with the familiarity of a spreadsheet. When we create a dashboard in *Chapter 8*, you will see the interactive power of combining charts and crosstabs on a dashboard.

In *Figure 7.4*, you can see the uncomplicated way of creating a new sheet from a chart in Tableau. To do this, simply go to the bottom where the sheet tab is and right-click. Once you've done this, various options will appear, including **Duplicate as Crosstab**:

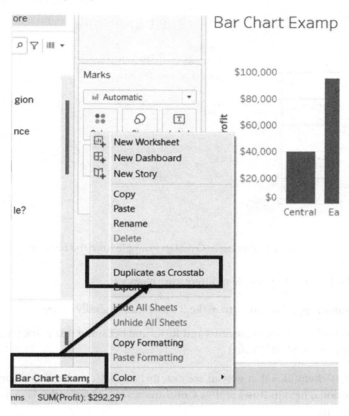

Figure 7.4: Duplicating a sheet as a crosstab or text table

Once this is visible, select **Duplicate as Crosstab** – a new sheet with a text table will appear (as seen in *Figure 7.5*):

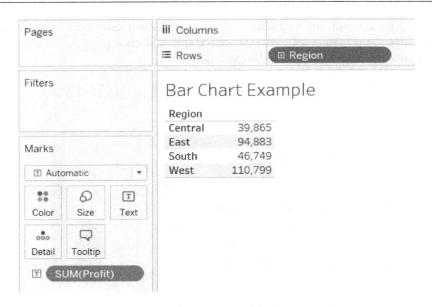

Figure 7.5: Duplicate as Crosstab example from the bar chart

As you can see, Tableau made a couple of interesting changes:

- First, **Region** dropped to **Rows** to make it more user-friendly to see

- **Profit** was eliminated from **Columns** and **Rows** and became a text mark (as seen by the **T** icon immediately left of **SUM(Profit)**

Something else that's helpful is that we can see exactly how basic tables are constructed in Tableau. You need a dimensional field in **Rows** and/or **Columns** and a text field (this is usually a measure, but it can be a dimension).

Now that you have a text table with a region, it might be interesting to get the values at the state level since this is deeper. **Region** is hierarchical because there is a plus sign left of the field (see *Figure 7.5*). Select this + sign to see the profit at the next level – in this case, the state/province level. This can be seen in *Figure 7.6*:

> **Note**
> Here, I have formatted **SUM(Profit)** to currency.

Figure 7.6: Adding a new dimension from a hierarchy

Even though all the regions are profitable overall, some states are not profitable as the default formatting of negative values is wrapped in parenthesis (or ()) as it is easier to see values in parenthesis compared to a minus sign in tables filled with data.

Since Tableau does not automatically show totals for tables and we have a lot of data points now, it would be useful to see grand totals for the entire table and region. To do this, you will need to specifically identify that you want to access totals.

To do this, you need to go to the menu bar, select the **Analysis** ribbon, then select **Totals** and then **Show Column Grand Totals**. I have also selected **Column Totals to Top** here. This helps me see the totals I want to see quicker when there are a lot of rows. Review *Figure 7.7* to see how this was carried out:

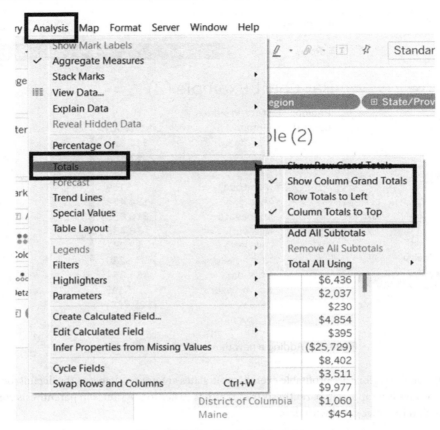

Figure 7.7: Creating totals for tables

Recall that I shared that we also wanted to see totals at the **Region** level. This will help you verify the totals coming from the bar chart. To view the totals at the **Region** level, you need to enable subtotals.

> **Important note**
>
> Subtotals can only be generated when there are totals. *Figure 7.7* shows a way to show all subtotals. Although it may be possible to show totals at every dimension, it is strongly suggested that you add subtotals based on the following examples for total control and to not confuse viewers.

To enable subtotals on **Region**, right-click **Region** in **Rows** and select **Subtotals**. The default format of grand totals is a bolder font with a **Grand Total** header; subtotals follow the standard text format and show as **Totals**. *Figure 7.8* shows this:

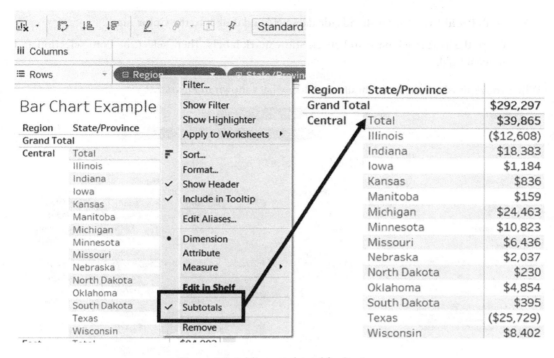

Figure 7.8: Adding a subtotal for Region

The subtotal for **Central** appears on top as the column totals were defined to be on top. For our next chart, please deselect **Show Column Grand Totals** under **Analysis** and **Subtotals** under **Region**. Our next chart will show a comparison of totals per state; here, totals are not relevant.

Highlight table (also known as a heat map)

A **highlight table** is best used as a text table, but colored cells should be used to highlight comparisons. If you come from an Excel background, you'll see that this resembles conditional formatting. It helps users find a context for the value much quicker than just going through the text. In addition, you will be highlighting profits by state for each product category.

For this chart, you are advancing a level. This is the hardest chart you have worked on so far, but you have the knowledge and the data to create it. The instructions to create a highlight table are as follows:

1. Right-click the table sheet tab and select **Duplicate** (which is at the bottom of the application).

2. Name the sheet `Highlight Table Example`.

3. Add **Category** to **Columns**.

4. From the **Marks** section, change the chart type from **Text** to **Square**.

5. Grab **Profit** from the left-hand side data field and drag it to the **Color** mark.

6. Go to the **Text** label mark and check **Show mark labels**. Then, select the **Font** selection and make it bold.

When you're finished, the table should look like what's shown in *Figure 7.9*:

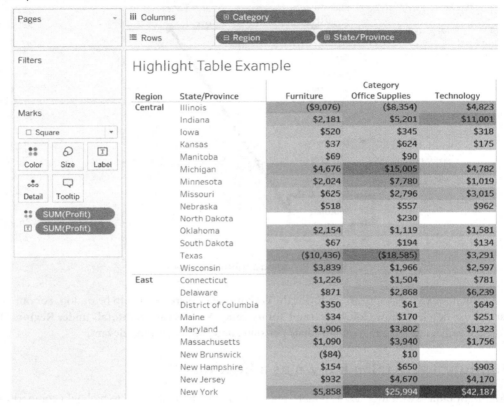

Figure 7.9: Highlight table example

With that, you have learned how to create a highlight table without **Ask Me**. However, to better understand the chart's purpose, you should review some interesting insights.

Interesting insights

Let us go over several interesting things that came out of this creation:

- The color scheme that appeared automatically was a diverging color palette. It came out as diverging because Tableau noticed that there were negative and positive numbers. The color scale would be sequential by default if the lowest number started at zero.

- Even though we had a text field in the **Marks** section, text did not appear automatically – this was because we modified the chart type from text to a square chart.

- The null values did not show up as text or color – this is because null values do not affect the color scheme.

- With the **Automatic** text font color, the font changes color from black to white, depending on the fill color of the square. Note that if your squares are too small, they will default to black regardless of the background color.

Why did I go into so much detail about how Tableau responds?

As someone who is taking a knowledge-based test, you will not have access to Tableau or the internet. Changing your mindset from a basic understanding of actions to why and how will help significantly improve your chances. To do this, I strongly encourage you to recreate charts multiple times to understand them. Creating them and understanding this process will undoubtedly help you answer the questions presented more confidently (and competently).

If you felt intimidated by the example in this section, don't worry – we will take it a little easier with the next one!

Stacked bar chart

A **stacked bar chart** functions similarly to a standard bar chart but looks at multiple dimensions per bar. This means a user can get more context about how a sub-dimension changes a value.

Notes

Stacked bar charts are more effective as they show no more than five dimensions; having too many is detrimental rather than providing insight. In addition, having sectional labels on bar charts to help find values is strongly encouraged as slices may be difficult to see.

In the following example, we will go over regions and omit states from the analysis – much like the first bar chart. However, I want to see how a product category drives profit regionally. The instructions to create a stacked bar chart are as follows:

1. Duplicate the `Bar Chart Example` sheet.

2. Rename the sheet `Stacked Bar Chart Example`.

3. Drag **Category** to the **Color** mark.

4. Go to the **Text** label mark and check **Show mark labels**. Then, select the **Font** selection and make it bold. You can access this by navigating to the **T** label in the **Marks** section.

Here is what the chart should look like when complete:

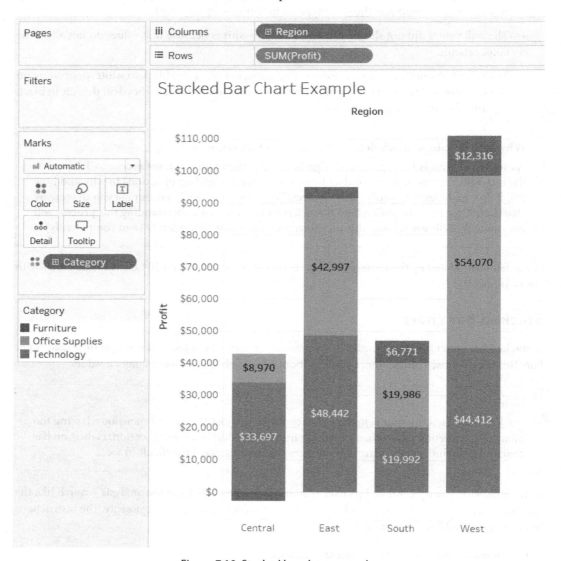

Figure 7.10: Stacked bar chart example

> **Note**
>
> I dragged the category legend from the right-hand side to under the **Marks** section.

Interesting insights

Let us go over several interesting things that arose from the stacked bar chart, as shown on the right-hand side of your visualization:

- **Furniture** had the least impact on profits.

- Although the **Furniture** category defaults to the top, it was at the bottom of **Central**. This is because it yielded a negative profit. Since the negative amount was nominal, the text was not visible in the screenshot.

- **West** had the most profit, but **East** had the strongest **Technology** profits.

> **Note**
>
> To verify the profit of a section, remember to hover over the tooltip. Any item shown in the **Columns**, **Rows**, and **Marks** sections show up on tooltips by default (unless modified).

Line chart

Line charts are simple but foundational charts. Line charts track changes over a continuous dimension, most commonly time. Let us create a line chart:

1. Create a new worksheet.
2. Rename the sheet Line Chart Example.
3. Drag **MONTH (Order Date)** to the **Columns** mark.
4. Right-click on **MONTH (Order Date)**. Then, in the popup that appears, select **Month** in **MMM YYYY** format (as shown in *Figure 7.11*). This option defaults to continuous, but double-check that **Continuous** is selected rather than **Discrete**:

Figure 7.11: Selecting Continuous and Month from MONTH (Order Date)

5. Move **Sales** to **Rows**.

6. Under, **Marks** select **Label**, which is on the **T** label in the **Marks** section. This will display a pop-up dialog box, as seen in *Figure 7.12* (see *Figure 7.12* to confirm *Steps 6-8*).

7. Check **Show mark labels**.

8. Select **Min/Max** under **Marks to Label**:

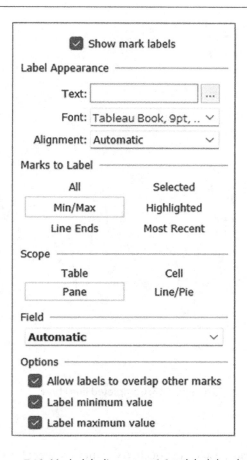

Figure 7.12: Marks labeling steps 6-8 to label the chart

Figure 7.13 shows what the completed line chart looks like after you have completed the preceding steps:

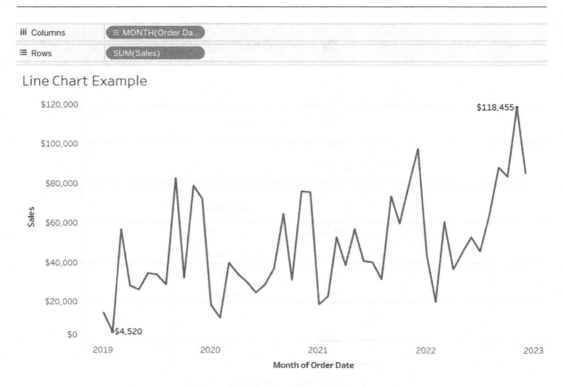

Figure 7.13: Completed line chart

Interesting insights

Line charts are one of the most used types of charts as they are great for showing data over time. Let us dig into what is useful in this use case:

- Sales have been trending upward, with a peak month near the end of the dates (2023).

- Tableau dynamically shows dates on **Month of Order Date**. This is because Tableau is smart enough to see that the date format (and spacing) is the best fit for the size and dimensions of your chart and the data it contains. However, note that the dimension is at the month level.

Area chart

Area charts are simply filled-in line charts or a combination of a bar chart and a line chart. They are of more value when multiple dimensions are shaded in, which makes them remarkably like stacked bar charts but without dimensional spaces. With that knowledge, let us create an area chart:

1. Duplicate the `Line Chart Example` sheet.

2. Rename the sheet `Area Chart Example`.

3. Select **Area** under **Marks** for the chart type.

4. Drag **Region** to **Color** in the **Marks** section.

5. Change the color palette to **Nuriel Stone** by selecting **Color | Edit Colors | Select Color Palette**, as seen in *Figure 7.14*:

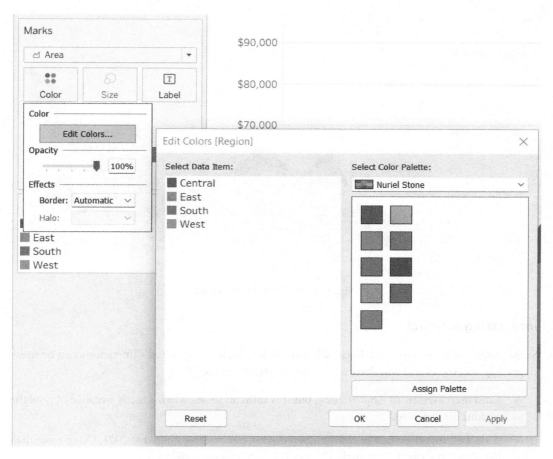

Figure 7.14: Selecting a color palette from the Marks section

6. Remove any text labels.

7. Add an **Order Date** filter, but filter to year = 2021.

> **Note**
>
> A simple area chart was created after *Step 3*, at which point it was a filled line chart.

When complete, your chart should look like what's shown in *Figure 7.15*:

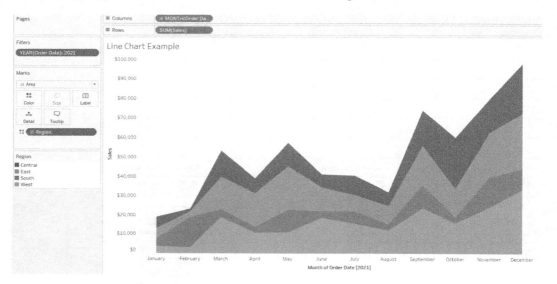

Figure 7.15: (Stacked) area chart

Interesting insights

Sometimes, use cases require additional context, in which case colored dimensions can be used. Regarding this use case, I will share a few insights that I can see:

- Sales increased from August 2021, but it is difficult to see when exactly because of how the regions are separated.

- A stacked area chart can be easily cluttered, so in our case, we filtered to 2021. Using more than five slices in an area chart makes it even less valuable for insights.

- The **South** region appeared to have the least number of sales (second from the bottom) from **March** through the end of the year.

Scatter plot

Scatter plots are analytically robust graphs that show a data point at the intersection of two numerical variables from a micro perspective. From a macro perspective, they are used to look at patterns and correlations between two numerical variables. Let us create a scatter plot:

1. Create a new worksheet.
2. Rename the sheet `Scatter Plot Chart Example`.
3. Add **Sales** to **Columns** (it should default to **SUM(Sales)**).
4. Add **Profit Ratio** to **Rows** (it should default to **AGG(Profit Ratio)**).
5. Add **Sub-Category** as a detail in the **Marks** section.
6. Add **Category** to **Color** in the **Marks** section.
7. Change the shape from what should be an open circle to a filled circle by selecting the relevant option under **Shape** in the **Marks** section.
8. Add a **Trend Line** by selecting **Analytics**. See *Figure 7.15* for a visual clue:

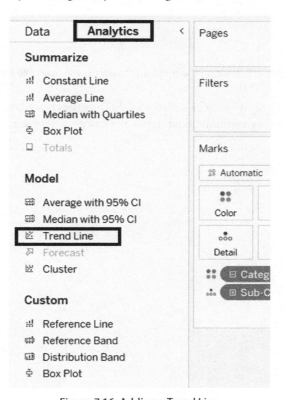

Figure 7.16: Adding a Trend Line

> **Note**
>
> If **Trend Line** (or any **Analytics** option) is grayed out, it means it's not available based on your chart.

9. Right-click on any trend line in your chart (there should be one for each category) and select **Format** (see *Figure 7.17* for this step and the next).

10. Change the trend line from a filled line to a dotted line:

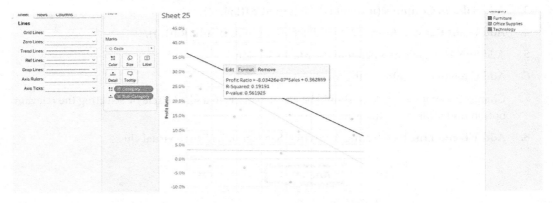

Figure 7.17: Selecting Format on the trend line to access the available formatting options

With that, you have built a semi-complex scatter plot showing the correlation between sales and profit with marks per sub-category and individual trends per category. Please see *Figure 7.18* to compare your work:

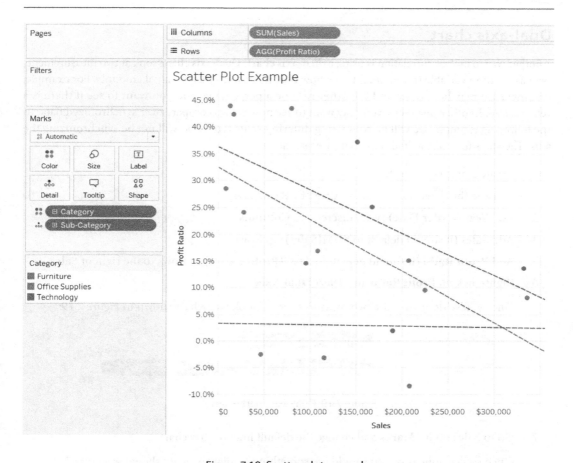

Figure 7.18: Scatter plot example

Interesting insights

Scatter plots can be difficult to understand for those new to data visualization but offer insights from being able to look at relationships between multiple measurements:

- **Furniture** had little profit ratio impact compared to **Sales** (as evidenced by the flat line)
- A higher profit ratio does not correlate with higher sales
- Although **Office Supplies** and **Technology** see a similarly reduced rate of profit ratio when total sales increase by sub-category, **Technology** trends the best at the sales points per sub-category

Dual-axis chart

Another way to look at correlation is using a **dual-axis chart**. Dual-axis charts look at two measurements over a common variable (often time) to see how they relate to trends or actual amounts. For example, one measure may be a value and the other may be a percentage, and you want to see if there is a relationship. In other instances, you may want to see how values compare over synchronized data. In the following example, we will be comparing differing value types and will not be synchronizing the axis. The steps to create a dual-axis chart are as follows:

1. Create a new worksheet,

2. Rename the sheet Dual Axis Chart Example.

3. Add **Year (Order Date)** (year, discrete) to **Columns**.

4. Add **Sales** (it should default to **SUM(Sales)**) to **Rows**.

5. Add **Profit Ratio** (it should default to **AGG(Profit Ratio)**) to **Rows** to the right of **Sales**.

6. Right-click on **Profit Ratio** and select **Dual Axis**.

    Once you've done this, the two measures should look like what's shown in *Figure 7.19*:

Figure 7.19: Dual-axis chart example

7. Go to **Sales** under **Marks** and change the default line to a bar chart.

    Once you've done this, you should see something similar to what's shown in *Figure 7.20*:

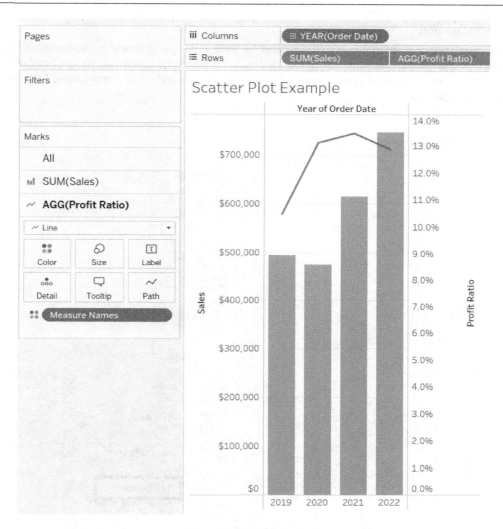

Figure 7.20: Dual-axis chart

Interesting insights

Dual-axis charts are also confusing for those new to data visualization. They are a little complex to understand as you will see two different measurements on unsynchronized axes. However, if accustomed, you can learn from the relationship or lack thereof regarding these measurements:

- Although sales increased in 2022, the profit ratio reduced in 2022 compared to 2021

- Although sales reduced from 2019 to 2020, the profit ratio increased

- There appears to be no direct relationship at this level between the profit ratio and sales

Important note

Although not relevant in this example because we were looking at different measurements and not trying to compare the same values, there are instances where the axes should be synchronized. To do that, right-click either measurement axis on your chart and select **Synchronize Axis** (as seen in *Figure 7.21*):

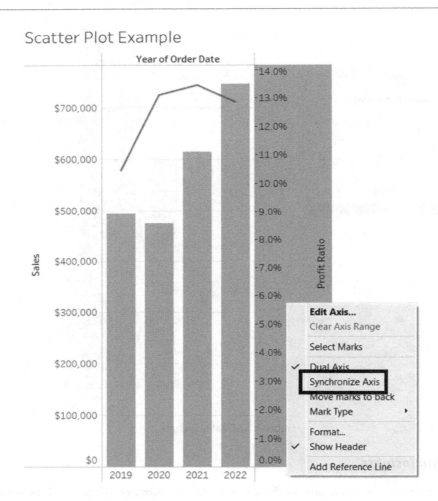

Figure 7.21: Using Synchronize Axis on a dual-axis chart

Filled map

Tableau has some incredible mapping features that create mind-blowing experiences for stakeholders. If you understand the available data, filled maps are easy to create in Tableau. **Filled maps** provide geographical insight when looking at a measurement over geographical dimensions. Let us create a filled map:

1. Create a new worksheet.

2. Rename the sheet `Filled Map Example`.

3. Add **State/Province** to **Detail** (notice how a map gets automatically generated).

4. Add **Country/Region** to **Filter** and only select **United States**.

5. Add **YEAR (Order Date)** to the filter and select only **2021**.

6. Bring **SUM (Profit)** to the **Color** mark.

7. Select the **Text** label and select **Show mark labels**.

At this point, you should have a filled map that shows profit per state and the value of that profit in 2021. See *Figure 7.22* for an illustration:

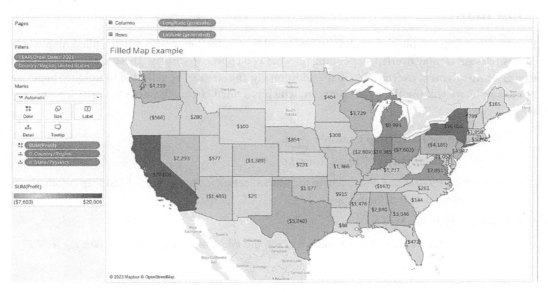

Figure 7.22: Filled map showing profit per state in color and values

Interesting insights

Filled maps do not account for all mapped use cases, but when there are good use cases, they are quick to create and easy to understand. Here are some insights that I've gathered from this map:

- California and New York orders were the most profitable in 2021, whereas Ohio and Texas were the least profitable – they had negative profits
- Some states didn't have any sales in 2021 and did not get colored
- Outside of the Northeast, there were no good indications of regional positive profit trends

> **Important note**
>
> Tableau provides many map formatting opportunities, including what to share with the end user and the type of map to display, but those items won't be covered in the exam; therefore, they won't be covered here. For more on this, please review Tableau's documentation on customizing your maps: `https://help.tableau.com/current/pro/desktop/en-us/maps_options.htm`.

Point maps

Besides filled maps, Tableau provides options to fill in smaller data points when a filled map would be less relevant or may overlap, depending on what you choose to display. These are frequently used to size a measurement overlaying a map. Additionally, the size can be reflected in unique shapes. In our example, we will use the most common, which is a filled circle. The steps to create a point map are as follows:

1. Duplicate the **Filled Map Example** sheet.
2. Name the sheet Point Map Example.
3. Drop the **City** field as a dimension in the **Marks** section (notice how the filled map automatically becomes a filled circle map).
4. Add **Profit** to the **Size** mark.
5. For the **Color** mark, reduce **Opacity** to **75%** and add a middle gray border (see *Figure 7.23*):

Figure 7.23: Reducing Opacity and adding a shape border

6. For **Size** under **Marks**, move the slider so that it's between the middle of the two hash marks.

7. From the **Map** menu (at the top), select **Background Layers**. The **Background Layers** tab should appear on the left-hand side of the visual where the fields normally are (see *Figure 7.24*).

8. Change **Style** to **Dark**.

9. Change the **Washout** percentage to **20**.

10. Uncheck the **Land Cover** option under **Background Map Layers**.

11. Check the **Coastline** option under **Background Map Layers** (see *Figure 7.24* to verify *Steps 7-11*):

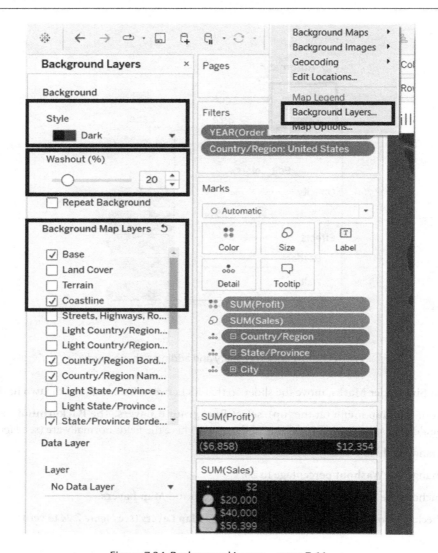

Figure 7.24: Background Layers – steps 7-11

Once completed, you will have a sized point map colored by profit, as displayed in *Figure 7.25*:

Figure 7.25: Point map example

Interesting insights

Point maps make it easier to see many details on a map, whereas filled maps are better for larger defined pieces. Here, you can explore more than just the state as a whole and see the specific locations for additional analysis:

- **The** Northeast and Southern California are sales-dense

- Larger sales volumes in cities do not always mean that they are profitable, as indicated by Philadelphia

- Reducing the opacity of the colors helps you see overlapping cities and the shape borders help the circles stand out more

> **Tip**
>
> For a deeper dive into the power of Tableau maps and adding additional mark layers, please review Tableau's *Help* section here: `https://help.tableau.com/current/pro/desktop/en-us/maps_marks_layers.htm`. Although it is not necessary for the Desktop Specialist Exam, it's a fun exploration of mapping possibilities in Tableau.

Density maps

In this section, we will not be able to build a density map because the dataset is not suitable for such a map. However, I will explain when to use **density maps** as they do have limited use cases. Having a filled or point map supports most needs, but sometimes, users require a density map to see data patterns when there are too many data points to display on a filled map. In the following sub-sections, we will go over the best use cases for density maps and learn how to build one.

Best uses for a density map

The following are two ways density maps can be used:

- Your data has a lot of data points that can't be read from a point map and correlations and patterns need to be seen that cannot be identified in a filled map

- You have specific latitudes and longitudes for each point and making a density map of larger geographic areas such as cities or ZIP codes would be misleading as that covers a land area rather than a specific location point

> **Note**
>
> Tableau automatically generates latitude and longitude for recognized geographies, which are either built as an area (filled) or a midpoint for a geographic area (point). However, for data in a density map, the data source should have the specific longitude and latitude assigned to the lowest grain of data (often an address, which Tableau cannot automatically assign).

How to build a density map

Many of the same processes can be used to develop a density map if you have specific locations rather than geographic areas. The data point should be an explicit location, such as an address. The one major change is selecting **Density** under **Marks**, as seen in *Figure 7.26*:

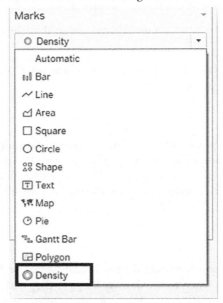

Figure 7.26: Finding the Density mark

In this chapter, you built 11 charts and learned when to use map types. While building these charts, you learned when they are best used, what modifications you can make, and what insights are available. It's best to explore these further, work out other scenarios, and consider employing more options to better understand how to create the insights available.

Summary

In this chapter, you created fundamental charts and saw their uses with actual hands-on exercises. You learned that these charts can be made without the Tableau **Ask Me** panel. In the next chapter, you will learn how to create groups, sets, and hierarchies to organize data. Then, you will learn how to apply analytics at the worksheet level via explanations and examples of sorting, reference lines, table calculations, bins, and histograms with an overview of parameters.

Knowledge check

To check your knowledge of this chapter, here are a few questions that this chapter's material will help you answer. The questions that have been selected aren't intended to trick you but to provide you with a learning benchmark to give you a foundational understanding to help prepare you for the exam. The answers are marked in italics:

1. How is a filled map different from a point map (select the correct answer)?

    A. *A point map uses a specific geographic point, whereas a filled map uses a geographic area*

    B. A filled map cannot display a value, whereas a point map can

    C. On a point map, you can see only some countries, but a filled map shows all countries from the dataset

    D. None of the above

2. Select all the options that are true about grand totals in Tableau:

    A. *Grand totals can be made for rows and columns*

    B. *Grand totals fields can be manually formatted*

    C. Grand totals appear on charts by default

    D. *Grand totals can appear at the top or bottom of a chart*

3. Which chart were you not trained on in this chapter?

    A. Stacked bar chart

    B. *Sankey chart*

    C. Line chart

    D. Dual-axis chart

8

Data Organization and Worksheet Analytics

In this chapter, you will learn how to organize data, use organized data in data visualization, and apply analytics at a worksheet level. Combined with *Chapter 7*, this chapter will provide additional information required for you to score 35%.

In this chapter, we will cover the following topics:

- Organizing data
- Applying analytics at the worksheet level
- Managing manual/computed sorting
- Adding reference lines
- Working with basic table calculations
- Understanding the basics of parameters
- Creating bins and histograms

Technical requirements

You will need the following to apply the hands-on learning in this chapter:

- The Tableau Desktop application. Most versions will work for the exam, but for the best results, use 2021.1 or more recent. The location of the current download is `https://www.tableau.com/products/desktop/download`. This version is not free but offers a 2-week trial.

- A version with similar functionality toTableau Desktop but is free is Tableau Public. It does not have all the data and extension functionality of the Tableau Desktop application but has everything you need for the Tableau Desktop Specialist certification. It is available here: `https://public.tableau.com/en-us/s/download`. If downloaded already, please use version 2021.1 or later.

- The Superstore Sales dataset. It automatically comes with the Tableau Desktop application but can also be pulled into the Tableau Public application by downloading it from the Tableau resources here: `https://public.tableau.com/en-us/s/resources?qt-overview_resources=1#qt-overview_resources`.

Organizing data

There are many ways to organize data in Tableau. For the Desktop Specialist exam, Tableau specifies understanding how to build groups, hierarchies, and sets. This section will provide simple, *how-to* examples for each by utilizing our dataset.

Grouping data

The primary usage of grouping data is organizing dimensions in bigger dimensional containers (for example, instead of 14 results, you may see the split as 3 distinct results). This is helpful to roll up data and categorize it reasonably for analysis. You will work on a group data exercise to learn how to create a group and subsequently learn how to edit the group.

> **Note**
> Measures cannot be grouped.

A grouping data exercise

In this exercise, I want to see the shipments processed by express versus non-express delivery. In the dataset, no field identifies that explicitly, but **Ship Mode** has the dimensions to help you identify that. This exercise will help you learn how to create and manage a group:

1. To begin, right-click on **Ship Mode**, select **Create**, and then select **Group** (the **Create Group** box will appear).
2. In that box, four dimensions will be displayed: **First Class**, **Same Day**, **Second Class**, and **Standard Class**. Press *Ctrl* and select **First Class** and **Same Day**.
3. With both dimensions highlighted, select **Group**.
4. Tableau creates a placeholder group name but shows an editable field. For the group name, type Express. The result should look like *Figure 8.1*:

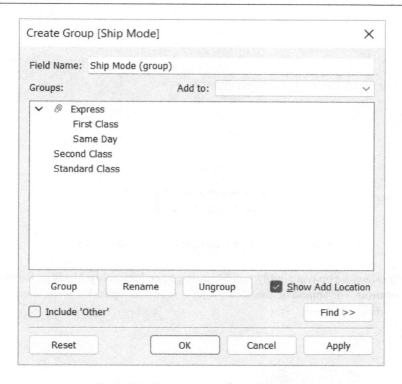

Figure 8.1 – Express group from Ship Mode

5.   Press *ctrl* and select **Second Class** and **Standard Class**.

6.   Select **Group**.

7.   Overwrite that group name as Non-Express.

8.   Change **Field Name** from **Ship Mode (group)** to Shipping Speed.

9.   Select **OK**.

Now, a new field should appear on the **Data** pane with a paper clip icon next to it, identifying that it is a group, as seen in *Figure 8.2*:

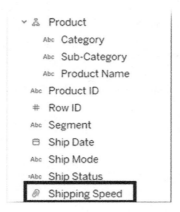

Figure 8.2 – Grouped field display on the Data pane

To test a grouped field, you can simply pull **Shipping Speed** and **Ship Mode** as **Rows** and **Orders (Count)** as **Columns**. You should be able to see what is shown in *Figure 8.3* where there is no disparity between the fields we grouped:

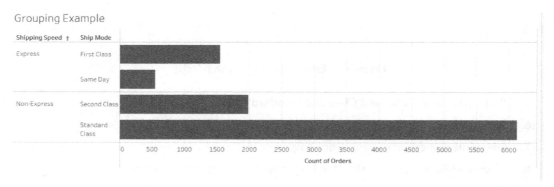

Figure 8.3 – Grouped field verification

There are less common ways to create groups, as follows:

- You can build a group by selecting multiple dimensions from a dimensional header in a table or chart and right-clicking to access the create group options (i.e., the **Shipping Speed** or **Ship Mode** dimensions in *Figure 8.3*)

- You can build a group by selecting multiple measures (or the bars seen in *Figure 8.3*) in a table or chart and right-clicking to access the create group options

Editing groups

You can edit a group by right-clicking on the grouped field in the **Data** pane and selecting **Edit Group**. Sometimes, you will want to edit an existing group – you will have to do the following:

1. Grouped fields act like any other dimensional field – they can be used for calculations, renamed, or deleted.

2. Individual groupings can be renamed or ungrouped, and new groupings can be created.

3. Individual dimensions from each group can be moved from one group to another, added to an existing grouping, or removed from a group.

Since you know how to work with groups, we can move on to create hierarchies. This group example is a prime example of creating a hierarchy.

Creating hierarchies

There are many occasions where users desire a drill-down effect for multiple fields. In Tableau, date fields have hierarchies built in, but other fields do not and need to be defined. A good example already exists in our data source (see *Figure 8.4*):

Figure 8.4 – Location hierarchy

In *Figure 8.4*, there is a **Location** hierarchy. The hierarchy is identified by the branched symbol. **Location** is not a field name; it identifies the name of the hierarchy. The fields in the hierarchy are shown from the top level (**Country/Region**) to the lowest level, which is **Postal Code**. Pulling any field above **Postal Code** into **Rows** or **Columns** will make it expandable. This provides the ability to drill down. For example, see *Figure 8.5*:

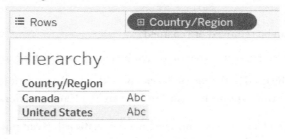

Figure 8.5 – Location hierarchy drill-down

Selecting the plus sign on the **Country/Region** pill or field will show **Region**. On **Region**, there will be another option, and if selected, the **State/Province** field will appear (and so on). This can also be accomplished by hovering over the **Country/Region** field name in the field label. Once the plus sign appears, it can be selected to dynamically show the next field in the drill-down. There is also a minus sign that allows you to drill back to a higher level.

Creating a hierarchy exercise

When creating the group for **Shipping Speed**, you created a field that naturally works for a hierarchy. There are times stakeholders may just want to see the data at the **Shipping Speed** level while others may want to have the capability to dynamically drill down to the **Ship Mode** level. To support this, you can build that hierarchy in a few clicks. Unlike groups, since the name of the hierarchy is not a field, a hierarchy cannot be named in calculations (but the fields in it can be used like any other). The following exercise will guide you to create a hierarchy:

1. Hold down *Ctrl* and select **Shipping Speed** and **Ship Mode**.
2. Right-click and select **Hierarchy | Create Hierarchy**.
3. Name the hierarchy `Shipping`.
4. Verify that **Shipping Speed** is above **Ship Mode** in the hierarchy (the result should look like *Figure 8.6*):

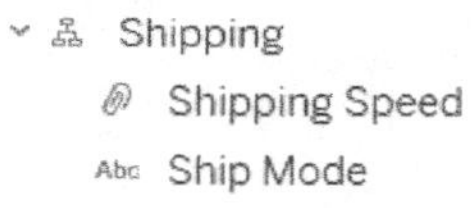

Figure 8.6 – Shipping hierarchy

Going back to the grouping example, you could now add **Shipping Speed** to **Rows** and remove **Ship Mode** to test the drill-up and drill-down effect.

Editing a hierarchy

You can edit a group by right-clicking on the grouped field in the **Data** pane and selecting **Edit Group**. At times, you will want to modify an existing hierarchy – you will learn how to do so by following the subsequent steps:

*   The hierarchy can be removed or renamed
*   Members of the hierarchy can be removed, new members can be added, and they can be rearranged
*   A field that will be used in the hierarchy can be added by dragging it to the hierarchy or right-clicking and selecting **Hierarchy | Add to Hierarchy | Name of Hierarchy**

You have built a group and a hierarchy and saw how the relationship can power a user to apply drill-down analytics. Next, you will work with sets.

Working with sets

Sets are custom fields based on a subset of data from an existing field. Sets can be used in calculations, referenced in parameters, have specialized actions, and can be fixed or dynamic. The following just covers the very basics of sets and doesn't consider their actions. The set icon is shown in *Figure 8.7* next to a set (a join icon).

The method shown will be how to work with sets from the **Data** pane – however, sets can be created by selecting multiple dimensions on a worksheet and selecting the set icon, but that is much less common and is not used often in the real world beyond quick or ad hoc exploration.

Fixed sets

Fixed sets resemble static filters. When creating a fixed set, you are telling Tableau to only look at explicitly *filtered* items on a dimension.

Our use case is to identify the sales volume of the top 10 most populous states and compare it to the remaining states in the United States in 2021 using a stacked bar chart.

I right-clicked on the **State/Province** field, clicked on **Create**, and then clicked on **Set**, as shown in *Figure 8.7*:

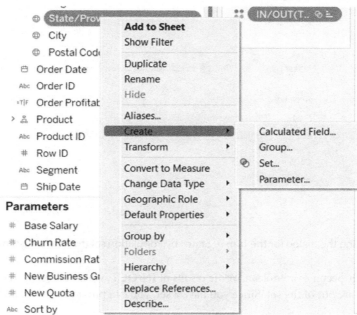

Figure 8.7 – Creating a set from the Data pane

At this point, you encounter the **Create Set** dialog box, which looks like the filter dialog. I went to Wikipedia to find US states by their population in 2020, identified the top 10 most populous states as of 2020, configured my visualization so that only those items were shown, and named the field `Top-10 States by Population`. After selecting **OK**, that field shows up with an icon to the left of it that looks like a Venn diagram. I opened the set again to verify that the correct states had been selected; please review *Figure 8.8* to verify:

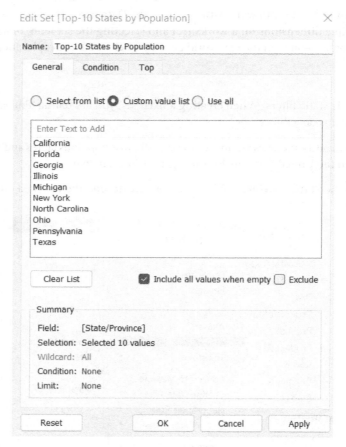

Figure 8.8 – Editing the dialog for the Top-10 States by Population set (field) in a custom value list format

This set effectively becomes a Boolean, or the results of **IN/OUT**, where the selected states are in the set and other states are out of the set. Since you have a set, you can put it to use and build a chart with it.

Creating the visualization

Sets can be used in visualizations like other fields can. You will be able to use that set to define dimensions in a chart:

1. Create a new sheet called `Fixed Set`.
2. Create a filter for **Country/Region** and select **United States**.
3. Add **Order Date** as a filter, select **Year**, and select **2021**.
4. Drop **Sales** in **Columns** (which will default to **SUM(Sales)**).
5. Select **Show mark labels** to show the sales values on the bar chart.
6. Add the new **Top-10 States by Population** field in the **Color** mark – it will default to **IN/ OUT(Top-10 States by Population)**.

The resulting visualization should resemble *Figure 8.9*:

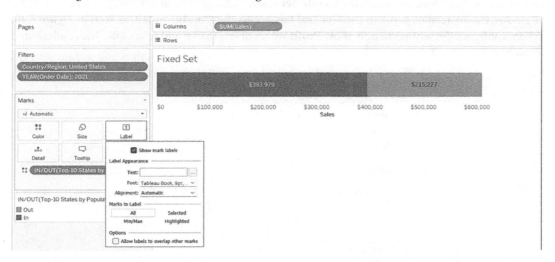

Figure 8.9 – Example of a fixed set visualization

Fixed sets are wonderful for many needs, but dynamic sets can extend the power of Tableau further.

Dynamic sets

At times, you may want your sets to work dynamically or based on a condition that can change dimensions. The most common reasons are looking at the minimum or maximum value to highlight it or reduce the number of dimensions shown to the most important ones.

In this section, we will see how to create a dynamic set to show the lowest values based on the data.

> **Important set notes**
> The ability to add additional calculations and apply context filters (as set actions are higher up in the order of operations than standard dimension filters) highlights the true power of set actions.

Dynamic simply indicates the set actions can change based on the condition applied. This set will be made from **Product Name**. To create a dynamic set, right-click on **Product Name**, click on **Create**, and then click on **Set**. Once you reach the **Create Set dialog**, change the name to Negative Profit Products. Instead of going to the **General** tab, access the **Condition** tab, as seen in *Figure 8.10*. Then, configure the settings to only show **Profit** values of less than **0** and select **OK**. The result should look like *Figure 8.10*:

Figure 8.10 – Dynamic set

Since you have seen how a dynamic set can be developed, you can apply this knowledge to building a chart.

Creating the visualization

Your stakeholders want to be able to see products with negative profits to make business decisions on what products to potentially eliminate. With a dynamic set, you can create a chart that will update automatically:

1. Create a new sheet called `Dynamic Set`.
2. Add the **Negative Profit Products** set to **Filter** and select **In**, which happens automatically when bringing that set into the filters shelf (you only want to see the results that meet the condition).

> **Note**
> If you select the caret on the field, only what is in the set can be seen when **Show members in set** is the toggled option.

3. Add **Profit** to **Columns**, which defaults to **SUM(Profit)**.
4. Add **Product Name** to **Rows**.
5. Select **Show mark labels** to show the profit amount.
6. Select **Sort** on the **Profit** header at the bottom of the chart and select twice to show the values in *ascending* order.

The visualization should resemble *Figure 8.11*.

> **Note**
> Please save this visualization to use in the next section.

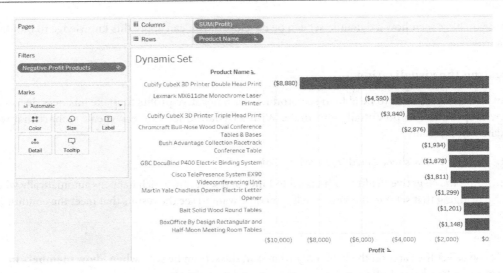

Figure 8.11 – Example of a dynamic set visualization

You just did a manual sort. In the next section, we will see how to add analytics to a worksheet, and you will learn how to apply computed sorts too. In the next section, you will learn how to add additional analytics at the worksheet level.

Applying analytics at the worksheet level

Tableau offers significant analytics in addition to building/displaying charts. Sometimes, only sheets are exposed instead of full dashboards or stories. In other situations, if analytics are added at the worksheet level, they can be used on dashboards or stories. In this section, we will go over some of the basic examples, such as manual/computed sorting, adding a reference line, basic table calculations, parameters, bins, and histograms.

Managing manual/computed sorting

Manual sorting means that sorting can be done on headers or axes by physically moving dimensions around in a field. This is what you did in the prior section when completing the dynamic set visualization. This type of manual sorting involved manual measurements. This type of sorting is also possible to do using dimensions, where you can physically drag individual dimensions up or down. There is not much more to manual sorting, and computed sorting is far more effective for dynamically controlling variables.

Manual sorting can also be done from the toolbar above the visualization. You either need to right-click on a pill and select **Manual Sort**, or right-click and select dimensions and select the sort icon, but that method is not frequently used. A **field sort** is powerful, as it does not require the field to be in a row, column, mark, or filter to utilize it.

In the following subsections, you will learn how to do dynamic sorting and also understand other sorting options.

Dynamic sorting

You want to make sure to be able to sort dynamically from the lowest to the highest profit. To do this, you will need to learn how to create a dynamic sort. The hands-on example here will teach you how to do so:

1. Duplicate the **Dynamic Set** sheet.

2. Right-click on **Product Name** in **Rows** and click on **Clear Sort** (to show results in the default alphabetic order by **Product Name**).

3. Right-click on **Product Name** and select **Sort**. A popup will be displayed, as seen in *Figure 8.12*.

4. Select **Field** from the drop-down menu.

5. Verify that **Sort Order** is set to **Ascending**.

6. Select **Profit** from the **Field Name** section.

7. Verify that **Aggregation** is set to **Sum**.

To make sure the results match, review *Figure 8.12*:

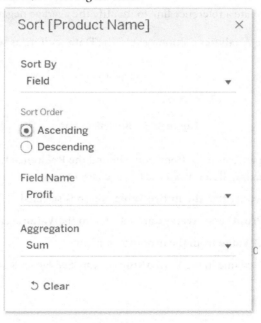

Figure 8.12 – Computed sorting by field

Congratulations, you created a dynamic sort! Here are some additional sort options available:

- **Alphabetical**: This is an A-Z sort, but be careful of digits, as it also treats digits in isolation, so if you have a dimension that includes 8 and 42, 42 will show up before.

- **Data Source Order**: This is the default data sort – it applies data as it comes from the original data source.

- **Nested**: This is like a field sort, but with the additional power of being able to sort in context. For more on nested sorts, please check out Tableau's *Help* page: `https://help.tableau.com/current/pro/desktop/en-us/sortgroup_sorting_computed_howto.htm`.

Besides sorting, an additional analytic component is adding a reference line to a visualization. Reference lines are foundational in many use cases.

Adding reference lines

There are many use cases where **reference lines** are used. In our use case, we will continue with the computed sort to see the average profit point for products with a negative profit.

Reference line instructions

In this section, you will create a reference line to identify the average negative profit for the chart:

1. To begin, select the **Analytics** section next to the **Data** section, as seen in *Figure 8.13*:

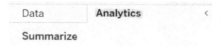

Figure 8.13 – Analytics pane

2. On the **Analytics** pane, at the bottom, you will find the **Reference Line** section in the **Custom** section. From here, drag **Reference Line** to the chart. Once done, a new dialog box will appear.

3. In the dialog box, verify that the **Entire Table** option is selected.

4. Verify that **SUM(Profit)** and **Average** are selected in the **Value** section.

5. Under **Label**, select **Value** from the drop-down menu.

6. Select the thick dotted line in the **Formatting** section. See *Figure 8.14* to verify the instructions from *steps 4 to 7*:

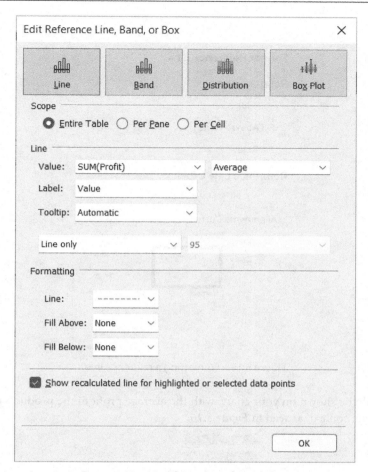

Figure 8.14 – Modifying the reference line

7. Right-click on the dotted reference line and select **Format**.

8. On **Format**, select the left-aligned, horizontal formatting as shown in *Figure 8.15*:

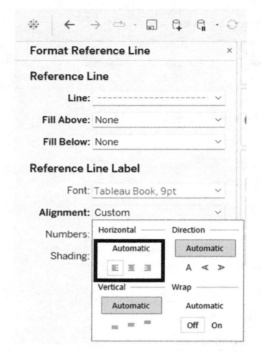

Figure 8.15 – Formatting a reference line

The result should be shown on your chart, with the average profit of the products on the chart to provide additional context, as seen in *Figure 8.16*:

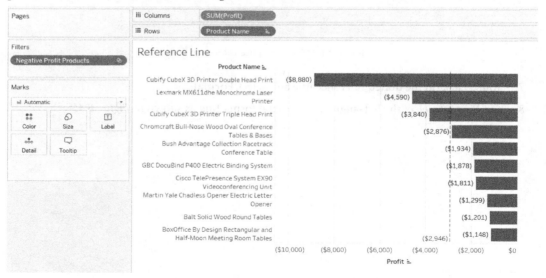

Figure 8.16 – Reference line example

Here are additional considerations when working with reference lines and bands:

- There are many options for reference bands and they can be shown at various levels of aggregation. Bands are a separate option shown in *Figure 8.14* – unlike a line, bands fill an area for which you define the start and end points.

- Reference bands can be made by following the reference line instructions as well; you can determine whether to fill them from beginning to end using a calculation, parameter, or other related value.

- Reference lines can be made at the table level (the most common form), per pane (if you have multiple dimensions to split), or per cell (or per bar in this case).

- Reference lines are also commonly used with dates.

- Reference lines can be based on fields or parameters.

You learned how to build basic calculations, so it's appropriate to enhance your worksheet analytics to understand the basics of table calculations.

Working with basic table calculations

Table calculations in Tableau are special calculations that allow you to modify the data to get the percentage of a total, running totals, moving averages, and differences. Table calculations can only be applied to measures (for a dimension to be used, it needs to be transformed into a measure – for example, **CNT[Dimension]**). Table calculations can be made in the **Marks**, **Rows**, or **Columns** section.

Basic table calculations are out-of-the-box calculations that do not require significant effort from the user to generate. They are made available by right-clicking a measure in the **Rows**, **Columns**, or **Marks** section.

There are so many options, but for the purposes of this exam, you will need to understand the following five options:

- **Running Total**: Provides a cumulative calculation rather than restarting every dimension.

- **Percent of Total**: Rather than providing the actual value, it determines the percentage based on the partition.

- **Difference/Percent Difference**: Determines the difference when compared to the original value that Tableau selects or you set:

  - For these, you can compare to the first value, previous value, next value, or last value.

- **Rank**: Rather than data values or percentages, **Rank** allows you to rank across a defined table calculation direction and by cell, pane, or table based on a defined value. With **Rank**, you can define the rank type by the following:

  - **Competition**: The highest value is 1, identical values are given the same rank, and values below the highest value are given their actual rank, so for five values, the ranks could be 1, 2, 3, 3, and 5 for values of 50, 47, 45, 45, and 41.

  - **Modified Competition**: Much like **Competition**, but instead of giving the two identical values in a list of 5 a 3, they would both be ranked as 4, as it goes to the last available rank number based on the duplication (e.g., 1, 2, 4, 4, and 5 – tied for 4th rather than tied for 3rd)

  - **Dense**: Works similarly to **Competition**, but instead of giving the last value a 5, it provides the last value a 4, as it's the next rank not taken, so 1, 2, 3, 3, and 4 for the values of 50, 47, 45, 45, and 41.

  - **Unique**: Provides a unique ranking for every item even if there are duplicates. In situations where there are duplicates, it looks at the order of the calculation to determine its ranking. The result would be 1, 2, 3, 4, and 5, even though 3 and 4 are the same in 50, 47, 45, 45, and 41.

In the following example, you will be able to create a table calculation.

Basic table calculation instructions

Although the examination will not go into exhaustive detail on table calculations, you need to apply hands-on experience to determine how they function:

1. Create a new worksheet called `Running Total Example`.

2. Add a filter called **Country/Region** and select **United States**.

3. Move **Order Date** to **Columns**. Right-click on **Order Date** and change from **Years** to **Exact Date** – the blue field should change to green (or a continuous date field).

4. Move **Sales** to **Rows** (which will appear as **SUM(Sales)**). See *Figure 8.17* to verify the steps:

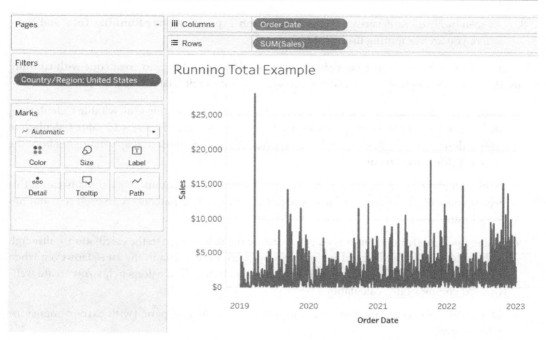

Figure 8.17 – Visualization example, pre-table calculation

5. Right-click on **SUM(Sales)** and select **Quick Table Calculation** from the menu.

6. Select **Running Total** from the **Quick Table Calculation** menu options.

7. Once updated, right-click on **SUM(Sales)** and select **Edit Table Calculation**. See *Figure 8.18* to verify you have accessed the **Table Calculation** popup:

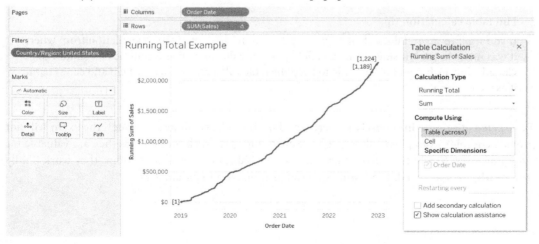

Figure 8.18 – Visualization with running totals

8. As seen in *Figure 8.18*, verify that the **Calculation Type** settings are **Running Total** and **Sum**, where you are computing using **Table (across)**.

Now that you have learned the basics about table calculations and how to create one with running totals, there are other options to consider when working with table calculations:

- Rather than creating a table calculation with full control by selecting **Quick Table Calculation**, such as the **Table Calculation** popup shown in *Figure 8.18*, you can select **Add Table Calculation**. This is done by right-clicking on the cell for **Add Table Calculation**. It appears right above the **Quick Table Calculation** option.

- Table calculations can be done at the cell level, which is not common, as in many cases, this leaves you with the original value of the cell or a misleading percentage in each cell, and has very limited use cases.

- Using **Specific Dimensions** allows you to define the fields to use in the calculation – although Tableau generally does a great job of guessing based on the data in the view. However, when there is more data, it's more complicated, and specifying dimensions helps you create well-defined complex table calculations.

- Depending on your data, you can compute at the table and pane (with extra dimensions added) level:

  - Across (as shown in *Figure 8.18* at the table level)

  - Down (which we may have used had we flipped columns and rows)

  - Across then down (left to right across, then restarting down at a defined level)

  - Down then across (right to left across, and restarting up at the defined level)

Fun table calculation tip

If you want to save a table calculation, simply drag the generated table calculation from where it was made to the left side of the data field pane. It will show up as a generic calculation (e.g., **Calculation 1**), but you will be able to keep the table calculation as a new field and can rename it as well.

Table calculations are immensely powerful and useful to learn about. Although the exam will not provide complex examples of them, you are encouraged to work on them, as they are valuable for work purposes. In addition, given their place in the Tableau order of operations, they work fluidly with nearly any filter used. Next, will be a brief introduction to parameters.

Understanding the basics of parameters

Parameters and using them are considered an intermediate to advanced Tableau function. Parameters are workbook variables that require a calculation, a filter, or a reference line to have value at the worksheet or dashboard level. Parameters can be boosted further with nearly unlimited use cases when actions are utilized.

The data types that can be used for a parameter are floats (numbers with a decimal point), integers (whole numbers), strings, Booleans (true/false), dates, and date and time values.

Parameters can be fixed based on user input values or be dynamic based on fields coming in from a data source. For example, a common parameter that is dynamic is **Date**, where you can modify the dates available based on a date field in your data source – when that data updates, so do the available options.

Parameters can be shown on dashboards and worksheets, but can only be used if they are incorporated with a worksheet. When appearing on a dashboard or worksheet, they look terribly like filters and are used in much the same way. The values displayed are dependent on the type of parameter used and its intended function. Next, you will learn how to create a bin and use that bin to create a histogram.

Creating bins and histograms

Bins are used to create dimensions for continuous measures (otherwise known as green pills). Bins cannot be used in calculations, but show up as fields on the **Data** pane. Bins are identified with a histogram icon to the left of the field name. Let's start by creating a bin from the **Quantity** field. See the bin icon in *Figure 8.19*:

.ılı.

Figure 8.19 – Bin icon

In this use case, your stakeholder wants to review the breakdown of orders by individual order numbers to see their distribution. Histograms are used to see distributions.

Instructions for creating a bin and a histogram

A bin is a field needed to develop histograms. In the following hands-on example, you will be able to develop a bin to be used in a histogram:

1. Create a new worksheet and name it `Bin and Histogram Example`.
2. Right-click on the **Quantity** field and click on **Create** and **Bins**.
3. In the **Edit Bin** popup, review the options.
4. Keep the field name the same (it should be **Quantity (bin)**).

5.   Change the **Size of Bins** setting to **1**. Note that Tableau reviews the data and suggests a bin size by default, which you can return to when selecting **Suggest Bin Size** (see *Figure 8.20*).

> **Note**
> Beneath this section, you can see the range in data from the minimum (1) to the maximum (14) value, the difference (13), and the distinct count (14), as Tableau looks at your data to help define this for you.

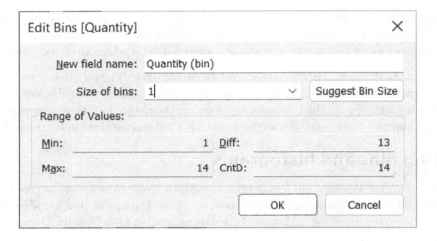

Figure 8.20 – Bin example

6.   Select **OK**.
7.   Move the **Quantity (bin)** field to **Columns**.
8.   Move **CNT(Orders)** to **Rows**.
9.   Select **Show mark labels** from the **Text** mark.

The result should be a histogram showing that the highest volume of orders falls between 2 and 3, with a significant drop after **3**. See *Figure 8.21* for the visualization:

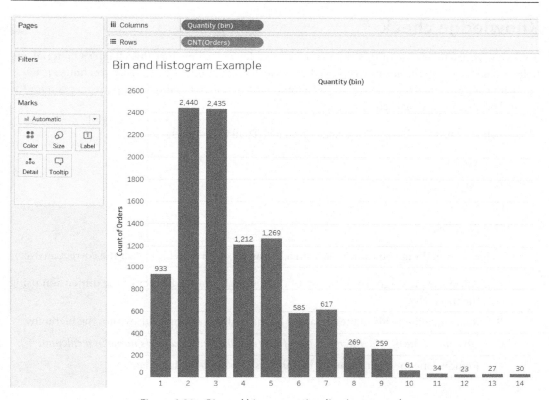

Figure 8.21 – Bin and histogram visualization example

Consider the histogram example a bonus chart. It provides a unique way to slice data where continuous measurements act like a regular dimension.

Summary

In this chapter, you learned how to create groups, sets, and hierarchies to organize data. Finally, you learned how to apply analytics at the worksheet level with explanations and examples of sorting, reference lines, table calculations, bins, and histograms, along with an overview of parameters.

In the next chapter, you will learn how to prepare your visualization to share insights by understanding the data shared in visualizations, how to format and create dashboards, and how to share data with end users.

Knowledge check

To review your knowledge of this chapter, here are a few questions that this chapter's material will help you answer. The questions that have been selected aren't intended to trick you but to provide you with a learning benchmark to give you a foundational understanding to help prepare you for the exam. The answers are marked in italics:

1.   Which items can be used in a calculation (select all that apply)?

   A.   *Groups*

   B.   Bins

   C.   *Sets*

   D.   *Parameters*

2.   What is something you cannot do with a hierarchy of three fields (select the correct answer)?

   A.   Select the plus sign from the top of the hierarchy on the header of the dimension using the hierarchy.

   B.   Rearrange the fields in the hierarchy by manually dragging fields within the hierarchy.

   C.   *Give the name of a hierarchy its own field (e.g., use the hierarchy's name in a calculation).*

   D.   Remove one member from the hierarchy so that two fields remain.

9
Sharing Insights

In this chapter, you will learn to share insights. Everything learned to this point has been primarily on the worksheet level. Tableau is ultimately a dashboarding tool for business purposes. You will learn how to format a visualization, create and modify a dashboard, and view and share dashboard data. The knowledge gained in this chapter is required for 25% of the exam's scoring.

This marks the final Tableau instructional chapter, so be prepared for a more in-depth, longer chapter. It's formatted this way as it covers the intended organization of the knowledge base for the examination.

In this chapter, we will cover the following topics:

- Formatting a visualization for presentation
- Creating and modifying a simple dashboard
- Viewing and sharing workbook data

Technical requirements

You will need the following to apply hands-on learning with the chapter's text:

- A Tableau desktop application. Most versions will work with the exam, but for best results, use *2021.1* or more recent. The location of current downloads is `https://www.tableau.com/products/desktop/download`. This version is not free but allows for a two-week trial.

- Tableau Public is a version that meets all the functionality needs of Tableau Desktop but is free. It does not have all the same data and extension functionality as the Tableau Desktop application, but it does have everything you need for the Tableau Desktop Certification. It is available here: `https://public.tableau.com/en-us/s/download`. If downloaded already, please use version *2021.1* or later.

- The Superstore Sales dataset. It automatically comes with the Tableau Desktop application but can also be pulled into the Tableau Public application by downloading from Tableau Resources here: `https://public.tableau.com/en-us/s/resources?qt-overview_resources=1#qt-overview_resources`.

- Access to a visualization in Tableau Public (`https://public.tableau.com/`) or access to a Tableau server/cloud (preferred).

Formatting a visualization for presentation

In previous chapters, you learned many of the skills needed to apply basic formatting to a worksheet, but without the context of best practice or in-depth finetuning. In this section, we will focus on more advanced formatting skills and provide best practice usage for the following, as they are focal parts of the examination:

- Using colors from the **Marks** card
- Configuring fonts
- Formatting marks as shapes
- Configuring visualization animations
- Changing the size of marks
- Showing and hiding legends

Let's get started!

Using colors from the Marks card

Tableau has two types of color palettes: one for discrete values (called **Categorical**) and another for continuous values (or **Quantitative**). They are segregated because data flows with quantitative measures as categorical colors are separated into individual segments. We will begin with categorical marks.

Categorical color marks

Categorical marks are great for charts to which you want to add additional context. On one end, you want to see totals, but also a breakdown per category. This use of color marks is common with many chart types. Your exercise will be the most common, and it is called a **stacked bar chart** (which you learned about in *Chapter 7*). You are also going to do one better and use a table calculation.

To do this, reference the grouping example from *Chapter 7*. In that grouping example, we created simple bar charts. Let's enhance that with the following exercise:

1. Duplicate the **Grouping Example** sheet and name the new sheet `Categorical Color Example`.
2. Add **Region** to the **Color** mark (now, you've made a **Categorical Color** mark on the bar chart).
3. Right-click on the **Orders** continuous measure on **Columns** and select **Add Table Calculation**.
4. Select **Percent of Total** from the **Calculation Type** dropdown.

5.   Select **Table (across)** from **Compute Using** (to verify, see *Figure 9.1*):

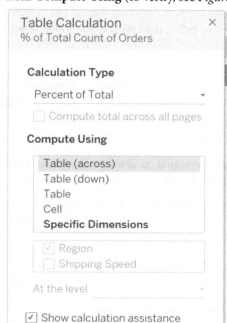

Figure 9.1 – Table calculation for percent of total

6.   Select **Show mark labels** on the text label mark.

In the end, you will have a breakdown of the percentage of total express and non-express shipments by region. See *Figure 9.2* for confirmation:

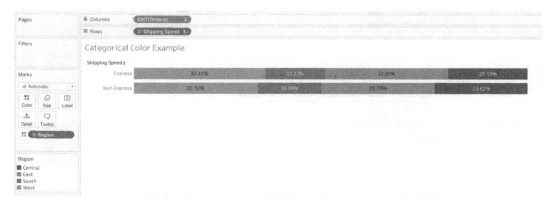

Figure 9.2 – Categorical colors by region to percentage of total by shipping speed

With categorical color marks, there is more context and insight that can be provided to your consumer than without. However, be careful to use them when they add to insight rather than distract, as having too many slices can cause confusion rather than insight. You will now work on quantitative color marks.

Quantitative color marks

Quantitative color marks can show values in color rather than marks. There are many uses for them and two different ways to apply them – they could be used as **Sequential** (a different shading of one primary color) or **Diverging** (which is using two completely different colors where the middle is typically gray). The difference between sequential and diverging is as follows:

- **Sequential color marks**: Sequential color marks are good when values will always be positive or negative, but you want to highlight the change in color (as shown in *Figure 9.3*)

- **Diverging color marks**: Diverging color marks are good when values range from positive to negative, where negative is an accessible form of red or orange and positive is an accessible form of green, blue, or neutral

In the following example, we will use the diverging color marks to show how to create something impactful, where bars show a value based on length, but the color shows its relative impact:

1. Create a new worksheet and name it `Diverging Color Marks Example`.

2. Add **Sub-Category** to **Rows**.

3. Add **Sales** to **Columns**.

4. Sort **Sales** from most to least from the **Sales** axis at the bottom of the chart.

5. Add **Profit Ratio** to the **Color** mark.

In the end, you see sales by product sub-category based on sales amount and additional insight into how profitable the product sub-category is. Review *Figure 9.3* for the finished product:

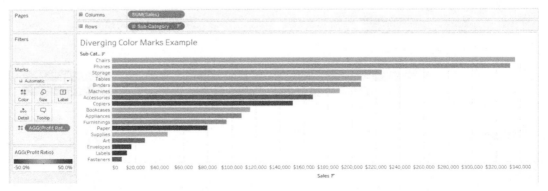

Figure 9.3 – Sales chart by category colored/shaded by profit ratio

If you did not want to see the chart colored by profit ratio and just wanted to create a chart by sales amount, you can press *Ctrl* and drag **Sales** from **Rows** and drop it in the **Color** mark. By doing this, you will notice that the palette automatically changes from a diverging one to a sequential one – Tableau is typically smart enough to determine the difference based on your data, but you have the power to decide.

You know how to create colors, but you, as a developer, have many more options. In the next section, I will detail the basics of color mark management.

Managing color marks

Although you can go with the default options, you can also override colors on Tableau. You do this by selecting the color mark section when utilized and picking whatever color you want. Any color mark that is selectable can be changed by selecting a color on the color wheel or color marks card, typing in a hex code, or changing individual color properties. Depending on your color mark type, you have different management options; I will cover each in the following sections.

Categorical color mark management

Categories can be colored by selecting a color palette and assigning a color to each category or by selecting individual categorical colors using one or more color palettes, as a user can select colors from more than one color palette. To manually change the color, you can select each dimension and pick a color from the palette to replace the previous color, or you can double-click on the color and a new color will be manually assigned. The customary options will look like in *Figure 9.4*:

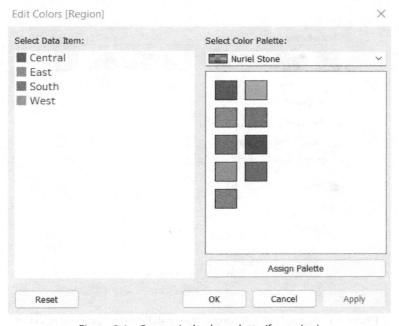

Figure 9.4 – Categorical color palette (for region)

> **Note**
>
> Selecting **Assign Palette** will select the colors from the palette automatically. If you have more dimensions than colors, colors will appear multiple times if selected.

Quantitative color mark management

As in categorical color marks, regardless of what Tableau preselects (diverging or sequential colors), it can be overridden in quantitative color marks also. Selecting the color marks allows for the following options:

- Selecting the palette type ranging from pre-made sequential/diverging palettes to custom ones
- Defining the number of color steps (great to control how the color appears)
- Reverse color range
- Use the full color range (helpful when there are a lot of potential colors)
- Define the start and end color range (advanced)
- Define the center value (great for diverging, especially when a metric or value needs to be *hardcoded*) (advanced)

Figure 9.5 shows **Edit Colors** for a quantitative color palette:

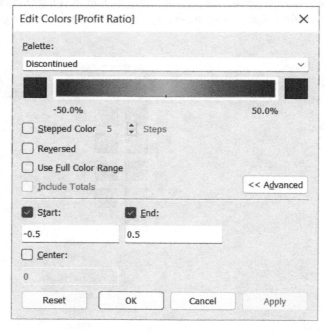

Figure 9.5 – Example of a diverging color palette with Advanced selected

You have seen just the tip of the iceberg when it comes to options for color marking in Tableau. There is so much you can do, including creating your own palettes and so forth, but that will not be part of the examination, so it will not be covered here. Next, I will cover font configuration.

Configuring fonts

Tableau has many options for font management. The default font is the Tableau series of fonts, but you will have access to your personally installed fonts as well on Tableau Desktop. Fonts can be formatted at any level, such as from the workbook level to individual pieces such as titles, subtitles, headers, and tooltips. In the following subsections, we will learn how to format fonts at the workbook and worksheet level and then see how to align fonts, and finally, go over a few important notes that we need to know about formatting notes.

Formatting fonts at the workbook level

At the workbook level, you can change the font type, font color, and size in the following listed elements independently of each other. You can access these by selecting **Format** and then **Workbook** from the menu. Here are the options you have for font formatting at the workbook level:

- **All** (means default for the workbook)
- **Worksheets**
- **Tooltips**
- **Worksheet Titles**
- **Dashboard Titles**
- **Story Titles**

See *Figure 9.6* to view an example:

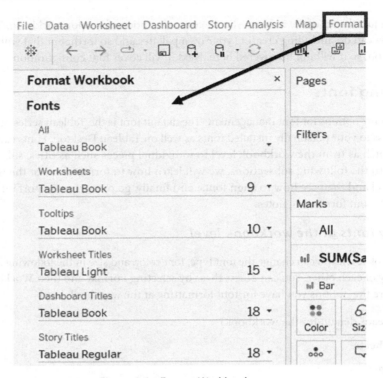

Figure 9.6 – Format Workbook menu

This effectively provides a default for font color, size, and type for the entire workbook. Although these options will also appear at the worksheet level, font modifications at the worksheet level can override the workbook default for the specific sheet.

Formatting fonts at the worksheet level

At the worksheet level, you have many manipulation options, which even extend to text alignment. To access these options, select **Format | Font** on a sheet you are on. As with the workbook level, you will be able to format the font type, color, and size. The following subsection will cover the available options.

Font formatting options

Once you click on **Format | Font**, the following options will appear:

- **Sheet level**
- **Row**
- **Column**

Each of the previous options is further broken up into specific options. In **Sheet level**, you have the following options:

- **Worksheet**
- **Pane**
- **Header**
- **Tooltip**
- **Title**
- **Total**: This is further refined as follows:
  - **Header**
  - **Pane**
- **Grand Total**: This is further refined as follows:
  - **Header**
  - **Pane**

The **Row** option has the following options:

- **Header**
- **Total**: This is further refined as follows:
  - **Header**
  - **Pane**
- **Grand Total**: This is further refined as follows:
  - **Header**
  - **Pane**

The **Column** option has the following options:

- **Worksheet**
- **Pane**
- **Header**
- **Tooltip**
- **Title**

- **Total**: This is further refined as follows:

  · **Header**

  · **Pane**

- **Grand Total**: This is further refined as follows:

  · **Header**

  · **Pane**

There is so much font flexibility but you need to consider several items with this flexibility, including whether the text is readable, whether it will render appropriately on the user's browser if published to Tableau Server, Tableau Cloud, or Tableau Public, and whether it's consistent/not distracting, among other items. With that, we will go into text/font alignment.

Font alignment

Tableau creates a default font alignment for all elements, which it calls **Automatic**. Tableau tries to smart-align the font based on the data displayed in your visualization. However, you have the option to override those options in the following ways. The general alignment options are found when selecting **Format** and then **Alignment** from the menu section.

The alignment options for text are **Horizontal, Direction, Vertical**, and **Wrap**. These options are further divided as follows:

- **Horizontal (text):**

  · **Automatic**

  · **Left**

  · **Center**

  · **Right**

- **Direction (Text):**

  · **Automatic**

  · **Horizontal**

  · **Vertically Upward**

  · **Vertically Downward**

- **Vertical (text)**:
  - **Automatic**
  - **Bottom**
  - **Center**
  - **Top**
- **Wrap (text)**:
  - **Automatic**
  - **Off**
  - **On**

The preceding options can be implemented at the sheet level for **Default**, **Total**, and **Grand Total** for both panes and headers, and at the row and column level for everything except the default pane. There could be default actions applied to tooltips, but they have the flexibility for font formatting on their own.

Formatting fonts in Tooltip

Tooltip is a powerful tool to add additional context to a chart. Text can be formatted independently with the use of dynamic references, such as the results of a calculation or parameter. *Figure 9.7* shows the **Edit** field for Tooltip using the chart referenced in *Figure 9.3*:

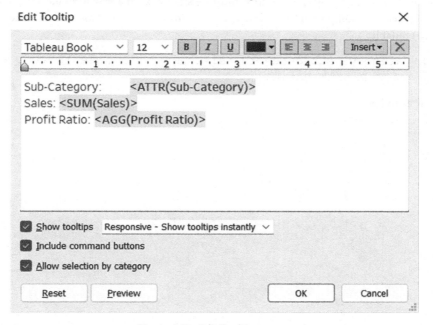

Figure 9.7 – Edit Tooltip popup

To access the **Edit Tooltip** field, simply click on the **Tooltip** mark in the Viz. Clicking on it shows its format. The format here (*Figure 9.7*) is in its default form.

Elements on top include font type, font size, bold, italicize, underline, font color, font alignment, insert (including other sheets for a viz-in-tooltips function, data source and workbook information, default caption and title, parameters, and relevant fields).

Using the options available at the bottom half of the UI, you can decide whether or not you want the tooltips to be shown and how, whether you want to include command buttons, and whether you want to allow selection by category (selected by default). You can also reset the settings to clear the tooltips, preview what it will look like, select **OK** to apply modifications, or select **Cancel** to cancel the modifications.

As you can see, there are quite a few elements that can drive the impact of tooltips. For exam purposes, Tableau does not go too deep on tooltips. However, I want to make some minor edits after looking at the preview (see *Figure 9.7*).

I want to change the default alignment to display the tooltip in a sentence format. I just want to make a simple dynamic sentence rather than three lines for every hover.

> **Note**
> The dynamic fields are in brackets (< >) and highlighted – the static fields show as general text.

To get the layout I want, I redo the tooltip with more static text in a way to make a sentence. To do this, I will replace the tooltip with the following, which includes more static text to make the format much more readable:

```
The <Sub-Category> sub-category sales were <SUM(Sales)> with a profit
ratio of <AGG(Profit Ratio)>
```

The result is as follows:

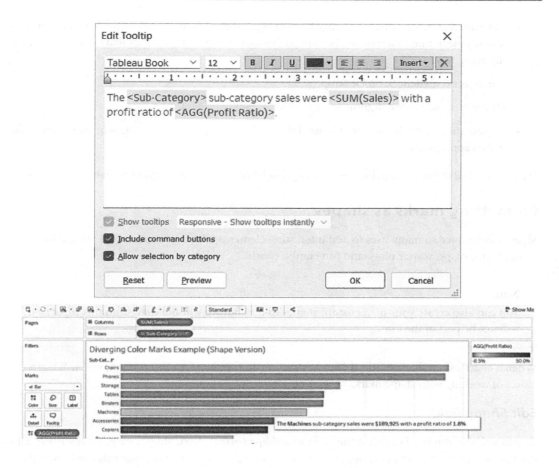

Figure 9.8 – Tooltip edit appearance on the chart

Tooltip editing is powerful and this is just the tip of the iceberg. Feel free to experiment with your tooltips to drive those contextual data stories – add supplemental charts and tables, and create calculations just for the tooltip to make them even more dynamic.

Other font formatting notes

You have learned the basics of formatting in Tableau, but there are more considerations and options you have for additional use cases:

- Users can click on dashboard or worksheet titles independently and format them in an editor that resembles the tooltip one, but with more limited options

- As hinted at before when covering formatting at the workbook level, setting default formats doesn't mean those formats will be applied throughout – they are defaults that can be overridden in many ways

- There is no spellcheck on Desktop

- There is no *justify* for alignment

- Automatic or default alignment is just Tableau's best fit based on your data – be sure to override when appropriate

We have looked at formatting, but now, we need to be able to format shapes on charts.

Formatting marks as shapes

Shape marks have so many uses to add interesting elements with more contextual pieces. They can be used with maps, scatter plots, and fun combo charts.

> **Note**
>
> You can also create your own custom shapes to use, but we will not delve into this topic as it will not be part of the exam.

When a chart uses a shape mark, there are ways to edit the shape. In this section, you will learn the basics of working with shape marks as the exam does not push beyond.

Edit Shape field

To edit a shape, you need to define the chart as a **Shape** (mark) chart. Shapes are generally made with discrete dimensions. In our case, we want to assign shapes to regions. Note that this works best if the shape is utilized on a continuous field.

For this purpose, I first selected the **Shape** mark, then added **Sales** to **Column** and pulled in **Region** to the **Shape** section. Once you have followed these instructions, you will be able to access something like what you see in *Figure 9.9*:

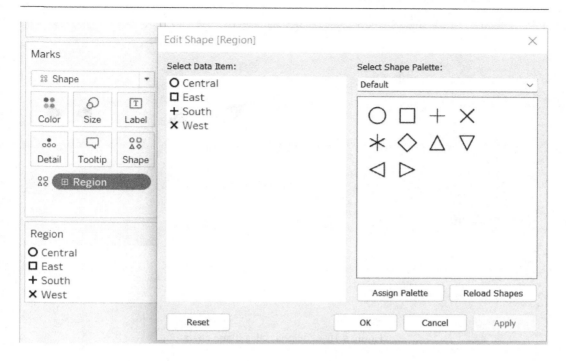

Figure 9.9 – Edit Shape access

From here, you can see Tableau added default shapes and there is a shape palette very similar to the color palette. There are two ways to change shapes:

- Go to any palette and assign shapes, but that is very uncommon if you have distinct shapes in mind

- Go to one or multiple palettes and pick the relevant shapes

For this chart, I manually selected shapes, as I want filled shapes that may best represent the regions. Since we have South, West, East, and Central, filled arrowhead shapes can work (albeit Central does not equal North but can be implied easily here). Let's see how to do this.

To access the desired shapes, select the **Filled** shape palette under the **Select Shape Palette** field, highlight the regions you want to assign the shapes to, and pick the representative shapes.

The other item I need to take care of is sizing the shapes appropriately. Sizing is done using the **Size** mark (covered later in this chapter). Once done, you will see a chart that looks like *Figure 9.10*:

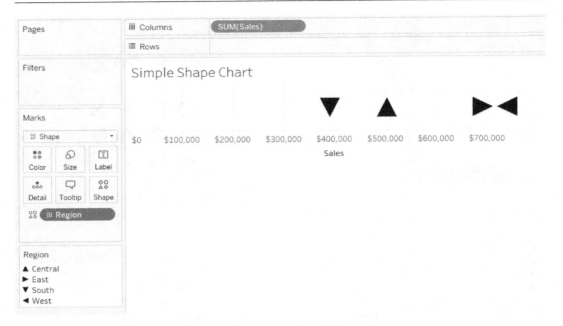

Figure 9.10 – Regional sales shape chart

Although this chart is not as simple to understand as other charts, it's evident the South region has the least number of sales and the West has the most.

> **Important shape versus circle/square chart distinction**
>
> The shape chart is different from the circle and square charts in that, circle and square charts are charts in the shape of a circle and square, respectively; however, a shape chart appears in the normal chart format but uses shapes to highlight the data.

Shape charts can be a lot of fun to work with and be almost playful, yet in other ways, add more context. Next up, you will learn how to animate your visualizations in Tableau!

Configuring visualization animations

Animations, specifically mark animations, are a newer Tableau feature, first introduced in *2020.1*. There are a lot of use cases applied for advanced storytelling, but here we will cover the basics of animations.

Tableau animations can be managed from the workbook level or by individual sheets. By default, they are turned on at the workbook level and impact all sheets. However, you can turn off or manage the speed and type of animation.

Animations are accessed by selecting **Format** | **Animations** from the dashboard or from an individual sheet.

Configuring animations for workbooks

Animations are turned on by default but can be turned off. The following list will detail the various methods to modify animations for a workbook and worksheet:

- **Configuring the Animation Speed for Workbook**: By default, the animation speed is fast or 0.3 seconds. Tableau has predefined settings of 0.3 seconds (fast), 0.5 seconds (medium), 1.0 seconds (slow), and 2.0 seconds (very slow). Tableau also allows custom variations between 0.01 seconds (1/100 of a second) to 10 seconds. Animation speed can be managed on the dashboard or sheet level.

- **Configuring the Animation Style for Workbook**: Tableau has two animation styles as of 2022. The animations use marks and an animation occurs when animate marks disappear (generally when filtering), movement (generally when a value changes size or type), sorting (when a sort is applied to a chart), or adding (applying new marks to the visualization). The default is simultaneous, applying animations to all marks and charts at once, or sequential, where there is a pause between the four speeds of animations (mentioned in the first bullet).

- **Configuring Animations at the Worksheet Level**: Although you can create animations at the workbook level, they can be overridden at the sheet level, so worksheets can act differently than the default workbook behavior for any combination of animations being turned on, speed, and style.

Other animation notes (as of December 2022)

The previous list covered the fundamentals of formatting, but the following covers other animation points to consider:

- Animations work on all web browsers except Internet Explorer

- Too many marks or pieces of data will stop animations from running, as it becomes a performance issue

- Some items – such as polygons/maps, text, pie charts, headers, analytical features (trend lines and forecast), and page shelf history marks – will not apply animations

Animations are a new key feature for engagement. They are not essential to visualization but can elevate experiences and storytelling when used properly. Next up, I will return to the worksheet **Marks** section to cover sizing.

Changing the size of marks

Mark sizing is a common requirement for data visualization. Not only is it important for pre-attentive attributes (e.g., a larger mark is easier to see when compared to smaller marks) but it also provides the flexibility to override the default Tableau sizing. Even though sizing can be applied to discrete and continuous fields, nearly all use cases and best practice applies to sizing based on a continuous measure. In the following subsections, I will show you how to apply basic and advanced sizing to a map.

Basic sizing

In a worksheet, there is a size slider that can be modified when a size mark is called upon. Now, I want to build a basic sales point map by state. Therefore, to activate it for my use case, we will follow the steps outlined here:

1. Create a new sheet and call it `Mark Sizing Example`.

2. Add **State** to the **Detail** mark. Note how a map automatically gets generated by Tableau, and **Country/Region** also becomes a detail and is added by Tableau, as it is based on the geographical hierarchy we learned about in *Chapter 7*.

3. Move **Sales** to the **Size** mark (see *Figure 9.11* for verification of the steps):

Figure 9.11 – Basic sales point map

4. The size of the points is too small for my liking, and when I click on the **Size** section of **Marks**, I notice it defaults to ~25% of the maximum size. I want to change the size to ~50%, or the center tick in the size slider. Here is an example of the size slider:

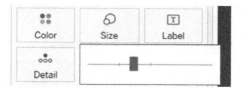

Figure 9.12 – Size slider example

> **Note**
>
> As of December 2022, Tableau only utilizes a slider without numbers for the **Size** marks section.

In *Figure 9.13*, you can see that it is much easier to see size variances:

Figure 9.13 – Point map with modified sizing

Most of the time, people do not go past this sizing feature for day-to-day operations, but Tableau does enable some slightly more advanced sizing options from size legends.

Advanced sizing options

Clicking on the **SUM(Sales)** legend carrot (upside down triangle) or on the legend seen in *Figure 9.13* provides access to another more detailed sizing feature, as seen in *Figure 9.14*:

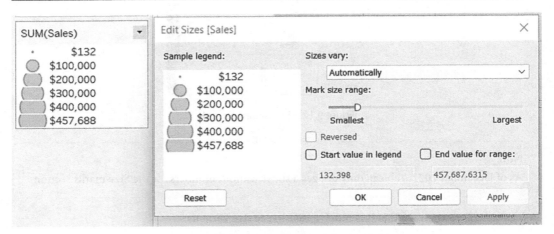

Figure 9.14 – Size legend editor (or advanced sizing)

The **Edit Sizes** option is a complex field to work with, but the following will cover ways to work. I will use *Figure 9.14* to cover the content of the next paragraph.

Sizes vary can be modified in multiple ways. The options are as follows:

- **Automatically** (a default sizing based on the data) looks at the data to see the appropriate sizing options and sizes from the lowest number (which could be negative or positive).

- **By Range** will allow the **Mark size range** slider (underneath the dropdown) to be modified based on a range (rather than the greatest point) and **Reversed** (grayed out in **Automatically**). This option is used when you understand the ranges or want to reverse the size based on values (where the lowest number is the largest).

- **From zero** always makes zero the smallest mark. Sizing is based on distance from zero (positive and negative) compared to the other data in the set.

With **Automatically**, only the sizes compared to the minimum can be edited but a user can change the start and end points by selecting and changing values in the **Start value in legend** and **End value for range** sections. Only **By Range** can activate the **Reversed** option or reverse the sizes from big when the lowest value, to small when the highest value.

Well done on getting this far with formatting. The last section on formatting is about showing and hiding legends.

Showing and hiding legends

Legends can be shown or hidden from a dashboard or sheet level. Since we will be covering dashboard formatting shortly, this section will focus on showing and hiding legends on the worksheet level.

One big caveat, as you will learn, is that your management of legends will not impact the behavior of legends appearing on dashboards, or vice versa.

By default, legends are created automatically when a sheet action results in a legend. This happens with color, size, and shape marks as well. Tableau fixes a legend on the right side of the worksheet. When adding that sheet to a dashboard, Tableau adds a legend to an open spot on the dashboard as well. You may be working with a lot of data with mark legends and may not want to see them on your worksheet. The following sections will help you manage legends in your view to see (or not see) legends of your choosing.

In the following subsections, you will learn how to manage legends by moving, hiding, and showing them on a worksheet (or dashboard).

Moving legends

You may not want to see a legend on the right side as that side also captures filters. Tableau allows you to move legends from the right panel by dragging and dropping between any panel on the left side (**Page**, **Filters**, and **Marks**).

Hiding and re-applying legends

Tableau provides two options for hiding legends (note that we are deleting a legend):

- Select the carrot to access the drop-down menu from a visible legend and select **Hide Card** (as seen in *Figure 9.15*):

Figure 9.15 – Hide Card from legend

- Go to the menu and select **Analysis | Legends** and select a checked legend (to deselect and hide) from the worksheet

To show any available legend when hidden, go back to the menu and click on **Analysis | Legends** and select the legends you want to display again.

You have learned so much about formatting – especially from the worksheet level. Next, we will learn how to put it all together in a dashboard.

Creating and modifying a simple dashboard

Dashboards are the most common delivery method for Tableau visualizations. Not only can you leverage one or more sheets but you can also have the bonus of interactivity between the worksheets to provide stronger analytical and exploratory powers than a single sheet can do alone. You will begin to prepare your dashboard, add dashboard actions, configure a layout, and format a dashboard.

Dashboard pre-work

Before you build the dashboard, you need to make sure the point map you built in *Figure 9.15* is complete. Your dashboard will look at a point map (with the sum of sales by state) but colored by **Profit Ratio** and further detailed with a data table or crosstab. To build a functional dashboard, sheets need to be added to it; the following instructions will show you how to achieve that objective by having multiple sheets intended to work together:

1. Duplicate the `Mark Sizing Map Example` sheet.

2. Rename the sheet `Sales and Profit Ratio by State`.

3. Add **Profit Ratio** to the **Color** mark

4. Click on the **Color** mark and make the following modifications:

    I.   Click on the left (or lower end) color and type in change the HTML color to #F17171 in HTML (select **OK**).

    II.   Change **Stepped Color** to **2**.

    III. Click on **Advanced** and deselect **Start** and **End**.

    IV.   Enter 0 in the **Center** field (which will activate the center selection).

Your card should resemble *Figure 9.16*:

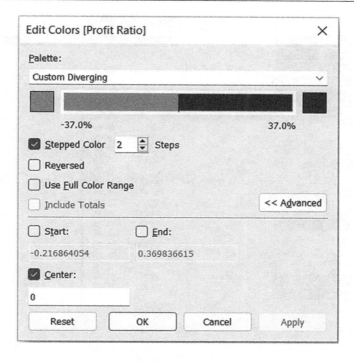

Figure 9.16 – Color editing

5.   Add the following filters by dragging them in the **Filters** section:

I.   Add **Country/Region** and **Region** and select only **United States**.

II.   Add **State/Province** and toggle to the **Use All** radio option.

III. Add **Sales(SUM(Sales))**, select **At Least** and type 1, and select **OK**.

6.   Go to the **Sheet** tab at the bottom of the sheet, right-click, and select **Duplicate as a Crosstab**.

7.   Rename the new crosstab State Details.

8.   Review the sheet and verify it appears as it does in *Figure 9.17* with the same filters (note that a new one was added automatically by Tableau for the crosstab for **Measure Names** to only access **Sales** and **Profit Ratio** measure values):

Figure 9.17 – State details crosstab

9. Remove **Country/Region** from **Rows**.

10. Add **Profit Ratio** to **Color** marks.

11. Right-click on **State/Province** in **Row** and select **Format**.

12. Change the default header font from the second darkest shade to the third darkest shade.

13. Save the workbook.

Now, you have two sheets from which you can build an interactive workbook.

> **Note**
>
> The initial workbook maintained the same filters as the previous sheet.

Visualizations and tables frequently work together in concert and provide a drilldown effect. For the next section, you will be able to begin the real development of your dashboard.

Adding worksheets to a dashboard

When adding worksheets to a dashboard, you really need to consider the layout for user experience. The more sheets you add to a dashboard, the more complex it gets. Furthermore, Tableau is one of the most complex dashboarding tools as it gives you the option to build sheets and then build dashboards, which allows for more dynamic interactions and looks. On the other hand, many data visualization tools make you build directly on the dashboard. Let us now see how to add sheets to a dashboard:

1. Select **New Dashboard** (🗗) from the bottom right-hand tab of the application.

2. Name the dashboard `State Sales and Profit Ratio`.

3. On the left-hand side, in **Sheets**, scroll down to the bottom and drag **Sales and Profit Ratio by State** and then **State Details** to the sheet. It should look like *Figure 9.18*.

4. Click on **Save**.

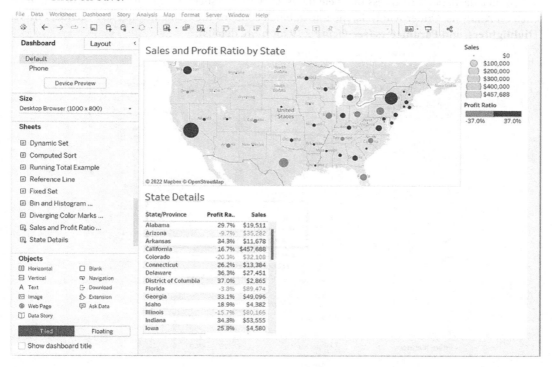

Figure 9.18 – State Sales and Profit Ratio with sheets added

Notice that the default size layout is 1,000 (width) by 800 (length) and that dashboards come with a **Default** and **Phone** layout. As far as the visualization is concerned, we can see the sheets came with the legends but not their filters. To apply filters and other actions, you will need to separately apply them at the dashboard level.

Another way we can add sheets is to format sheets on a dashboard. The **State Details** sheet looks fine, but we can change the layout based on preferences.

Adding interactive elements on dashboards

A dashboard's magical property for a business end user is its ability to work with other sheets interactivity to unlock insights not otherwise available. Tableau provides heaps of interactive opportunities to access on your dashboards. In this section, we will only find out where the elements are.

When on a dashboard, to access these elements, click on the sheet to activate the elements and then click on **Analysis**. Under **Analysis**, the fourth block contains the elements, that is, **Legends**, **Filters**, **Highlighters**, and **Parameters** (see *Figure 9.19* for more details):

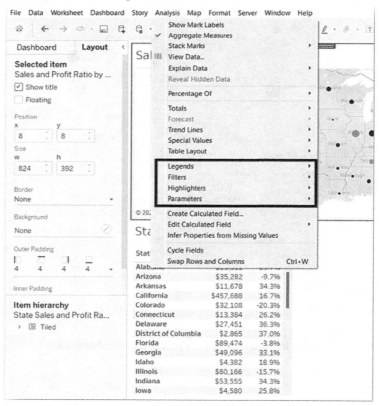

Figure 9.19 – Interactive dashboard menu

We will now see how to apply/add legends and filters to the sheet. Although you have legends on your dashboard from pulling the sheets over, you can learn about the controls for the **Analysis** menu. If you select and highlight the **Sales and Profit Ratio by State** sheet on the dashboard, click on **Analysis**, and then click on **Legends**, you will see that **Color Legend (Profit Ratio)** and **Size Legend (Sales)** are selected. If you don't want them to stay on the dashboard, you can deselect one or all of the legends to remove them. However, this way of removing legend on the dashboard is highly uncommon. Mostly, people directly click **X** on the dashboard itself to remove it. But this way is very useful if the users want the legend back on the dashboard.

See *Figure 9.20* for its display in Tableau:

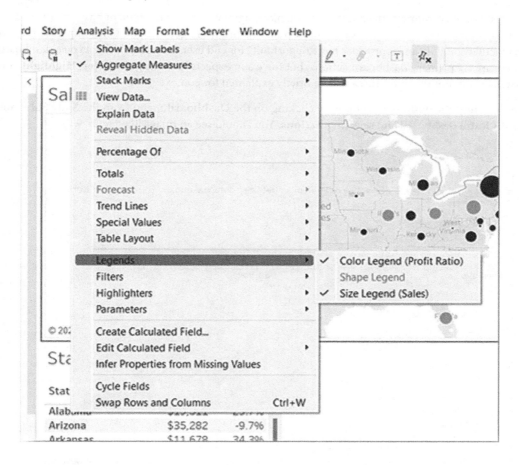

Figure 9.20 – Accessing legend options from the dashboard

Adding filters will require additional work, as they do not get added directly. You will need to add **Region**, **State/Province**, and **Sales** to the dashboard. To add the filters to the dashboard, make sure a sheet is activated, access the **Analysis** menu, and select **Filters** (very similar to accessing legends). You will see that no filters are selected. Simply click on the filter you want to add. You can apply this technique to any of the available options for filters, highlighters, and legends. Parameters work differently as they are not worksheet dependent.

Next, you will learn how to apply actions to a dashboard.

Adding dashboard actions

To dashboard consumers, these actions work like magic. When a chart element has something done with a click or hover or appears on a tooltip menu, end users get intrigued and impressed by the interactivity built in, and it provides more opportunity for end users to explore the data on a dashboard. There are six primary dashboard actions, but the exam expects knowledge of **Filter**, **Highlight**, and **URL** actions, but the other three will be briefly explained for context.

You will find the dashboard actions by clicking on the **Dashboard** menu from the **State Sales and Profit Ratio** dashboard and selecting **Actions**. You should see an image like *Figure 9.21*:

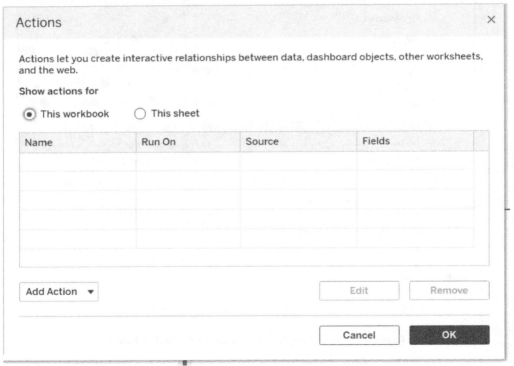

Figure 9.21 – Dashboard Actions menu

From this menu, you can add one of six actions. We will discuss the following three actions in detail, as they are necessary for the examination:

- **Filter actions**

- **Highlight actions**

- **URL actions**

Following this, we will briefly go over the other three actions, as they are good to know.

Filter actions

Filter actions work by filtering data between worksheets, so when the action is generated, you can see the impact it has on one or more other sheets on a dashboard. This is something that is common when working between charts and tables. If a mark is selected on a chart, it makes sense for the chart to show only that data on the corresponding sheet. Without a filter action, if the **California** mark is selected, then nothing changes with the table. However, when filter actions are applied, we can restrict the corresponding table to only **California**, which is a lot more intuitive for a dashboard consumer. *Figure 9.22* shows a filter action from the **State Sales and Profit Ratio** dashboard:

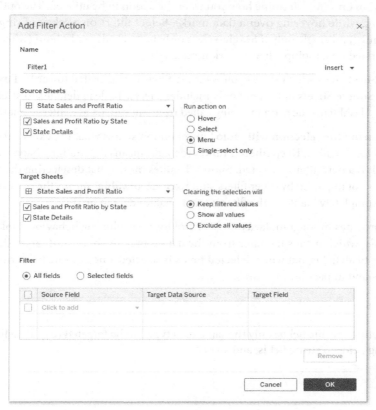

Figure 9.22 – Add Filter Action menu

To understand the **Add Filter Action** options, I will break them down for you as follows:

- **Name** is the naming option for your filter. It defaults to **Filter #** based on the number of filters used on a dashboard. Typically, a user would type over the filter to explain what the filter is, but can also pull from variable names by clicking on the **Insert** option to the right of **Name**.

> **Note**
> The variable names option would likely not be something necessary for the examination.

- **Source Sheets** are the data source, dashboards (with selectable sheets), or individual sheets you want the filter to be sourced from. By default, Tableau will show the sheets on the dashboard the action is being called on.

> **Note**
> Source sheets are a bit misleading because they encompass sheets and data sources.

- **Run action on** is to determine how you want the action to be utilized. The options are **Hover** (or acting while hovering over a data mark), **Select** filters on a select of single or multiple views only (and single only if **Single-select only** is checked); and **Menu** (where the filter will be generated on a tooltip when a mark is selected).
- **Target Sheets** tells which sheets you want the filter to be directed toward. **Target Sheets** looks like the **Source Sheets** option but only includes sheets. Tableau defaults to selecting all sheets from the dashboard the action is being called from but can act as a filter to another dashboard.
- The **Clearing the selection will** radio button option shares what the expected action is when you deselect the filter. **Keep filtered values** (default) means that nothing happens to the filtered data unless a new filter is selected; **Show all values** means that deselecting the filter will show all values not impacted by other filters; and **Exclude all values** means the corresponding sheets will be completely blank, as the filter is what enables data to be shown.
- **Filter** provides more granularity and control for your filtering behavior. Tableau defaults to **All fields**, which means the filter from the data source or sheets and target sheets will apply the filter to all fields, but when **Selected fields** is selected, one or more fields can be the source to target and impact how it works.

> **Note**
> When selecting specific fields, only the same data type can be targeted (e.g., date fields to date fields, string fields to string fields, and so on).

Highlight actions

Unlike filtering, highlighting does not restrict data in the view but promotes the visibility of what is being highlighted, while dimming the other data that the highlight is not applied to. The **Highlight Actions** menu is very similar and a little less detailed than the **Filter Action** menu, as seen in *Figure 9.23*:

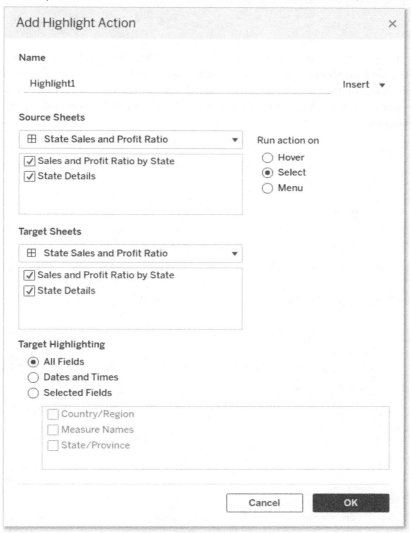

Figure 9.23 – Highlight Actions menu

Like the **Filter** menu, you have **Name** (and **Insert**), **Source Sheets**, **Run Action On**, and **Target Sheets**, which work very much the same. The main difference is **Target Highlighting**, which has similarities to **Filter** but is still slightly different. **Target Highlighting** defaults to **All Fields** like the **Filter** menu, but you can specify so that it only targets related dates and times and provides a finite list of selected fields that can be identified.

URL actions

A URL action is an action you can define on a dashboard that allows a user to access a web-based file outside the Tableau application. It can do many things, including generating an email or even opening a web object on the dashboard. You only need to know the very basics for the purpose of this examination but it is worthwhile exploring the power URL actions if interested. *Figure 9.24* shows the **URL Action** menu:

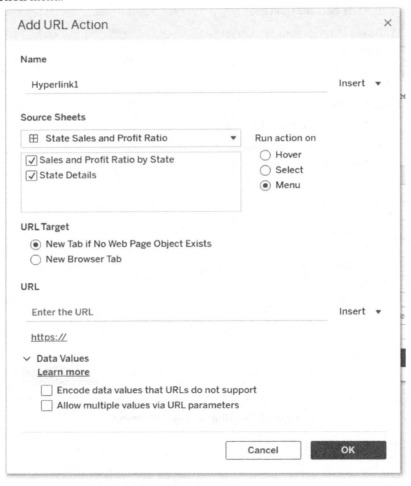

Figure 9.24 – URL Actions menu

Like the **Filter** and **Highlight** action menus, **Name** (and **Insert**), **Source Sheets**, and **Run action on** function in the same way. However, the changes occur once we reach the **URL Target** section:

- **URL Target** instructs you to open a new tab only if no web page object exists (default) or to always open a new browser tab. If you have a web object in your dashboard, then it will update that object, otherwise, open in a browser tab.

- In the **URL** field, you can enter a static website, static text, a parameter, or a field name (must use < > around these field names). Often, in these situations, there is a URL in the data source or a piece of URL as a unique identifier. When there is a full **URL** field in your data source, just add it as `<URL Field>`, and that can be the full text (if it includes its full web address). In other situations, the **URL** field may only include the unique identifier or the end of a website address. In that case, you can add the precursor, as follows: `www.website.com/<dynamic field>`.

> **Note**
>
> `https` is an automated precursor to any web address added, so do not include it with your web addresses. Also, there is a clickable test hyperlink that shows under the **Text** field. Finally, **URL Action** is also a common feature that is used to manipulate web objects on a dashboard. Web objects are embedded web pages that can be used on Tableau dashboards.

- **Data Values** are advanced options that you do not need to know, as they are not a part of the examination. However, they are good to know anyway. Hence the explanation of the options goes like this: **Encode data values that URLs do not support** means that you can add values in the text that browsers don't understand but allows your browser to translate, and **Allow multiple values via URL parameters** means you can access multiple values by defining its delimiter and its delimiter escape character.

URL actions provide more actions of use outside of the dashboard that give the users a wow factor under the right situations. Next up, we are briefly going to cover the remaining actions that won't be covered in the examination, but are helpful to learn.

Other dashboard actions

The following are the other dashboard actions that are good for you to know about from a knowledge perspective:

- **Go to Sheet** is a navigation action that allows a user to access a sheet or separate dashboard via a selection, hover, or menu item

- **Change Parameter** provides the ability to change parameter values via a selection, hover, or menu item when interacting with a visualization

- **Change Set** gives you the opportunity to manipulate a set via a selection, hover, or menu item (or deselecting) when interacting with a visualization

I have covered quite a bit of data on dashboard actions without providing an example. That will change now. On your dashboard, you need to provide a filter action from the map and a highlight action from the sheet to provide clear insight to your stakeholders when interacting with the visualization.

In the following sections, you will modify your dashboard with filter and highlight actions to make an intuitive and practical application that will work *magically* for your stakeholders.

Modifying your dashboard using the Filter action

First, we want to create a filter action from the map to the table beneath it. This will allow users to see what's relevant in the underlying table. I also want to make sure the full table is available once the filter has been cleared. Let's begin:

1. Go to the **Dashboard** menu and select **Actions**.
2. Select **Add Action** from the **Actions** popup.
3. Select **Filter**.
4. Rename **Filter** from `Filter 1` to `Map Filter`.
5. For **Source Sheets**, make sure only **Sales and Profit Ratio by State** is selected.
6. For **Run action on**, select **Select**.
7. For **Target Sheets**, select only **State Details**.
8. Select **Show all values** in the **Clearing the selection will** section.
9. In the **Filter** field, select **All fields**.
10. Click on **OK**.

Your filter action options should look like *Figure 9.25*:

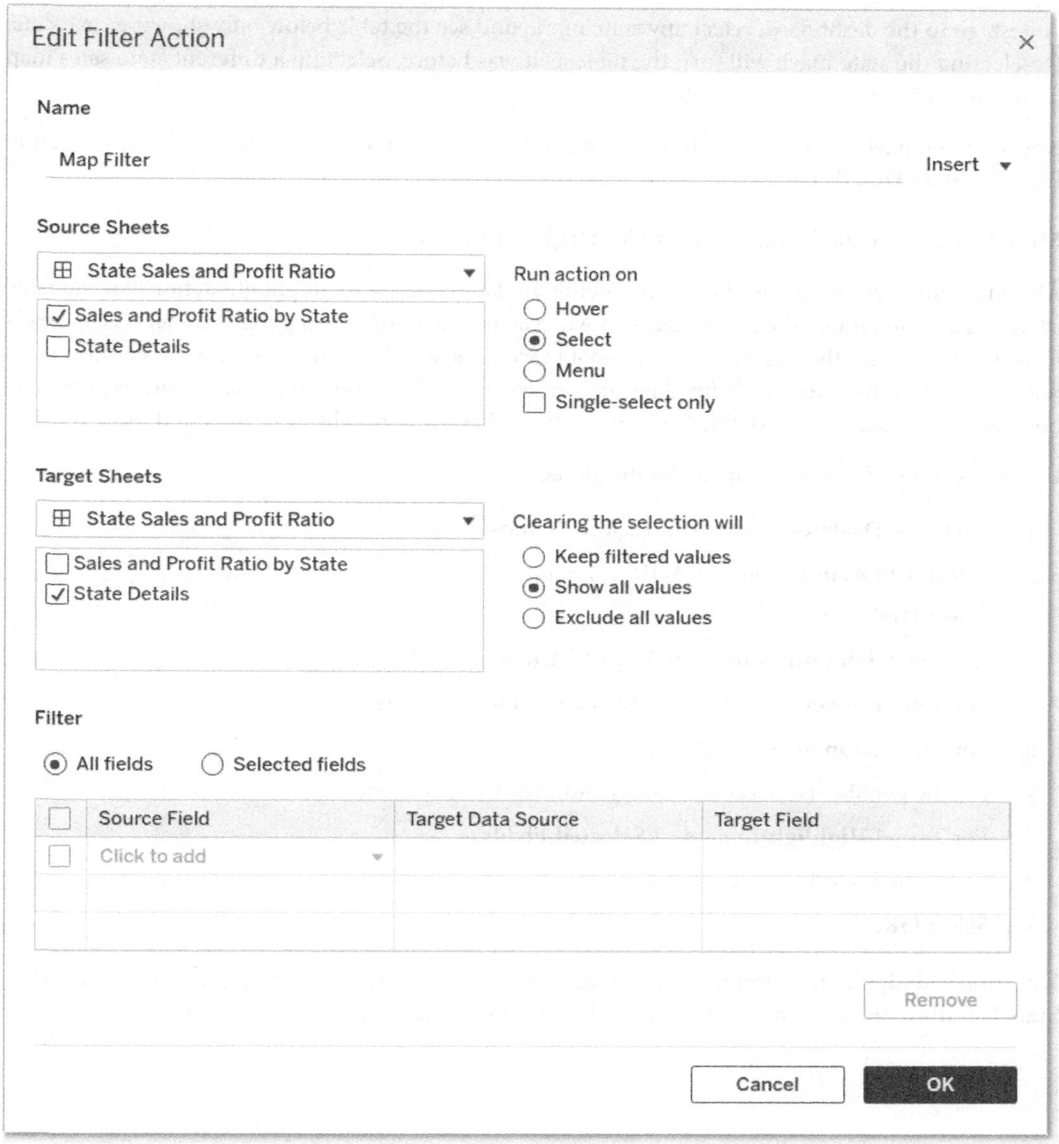

Figure 9.25 – Completed action filter

To test, go to the dashboard, select any state mark, and see the table below only showing that state. Deselecting the state mark will turn the table as it was before. Selecting a different state sales map point will refilter to the selected state.

Now that you have completed the filter action, you can even do more by creating a highlight action from the **State Details** table.

Modifying your dashboard using the Highlight action

Although filter actions get used more frequently in day-to-day work, highlight actions are valuable under certain situations. The best situation is when all the data from the highlighted sheets is in view – it can be confusing if the highlighted data is not in view and a stakeholder looks at a muted sheet. Also note that highlighters are a little finickier to work with than filters once your dashboard is published on a server, so being able to define fields explicitly makes the highlighting cleaner and more reliable.

Let us now look at how to apply the **Highlight** action:

1. Go to the **Dashboard** menu and select **Actions**.
2. Select **Add Action** from the **Actions** popup.
3. Select **Highlight**.
4. Rename **Highlight** from Highlight 1 to State Highlight.
5. For **Source Sheets**, make sure only **State Details** is selected.
6. For **Run action on**, select **Hover**.
7. For **Target Sheets**, select only **Sales and Profit Ratio by State**.
8. For **Target Highlighting**, select **Selected Fields**.
9. Select the **State/Province** field.
10. Select **OK**.

Your finished highlight action should look like *Figure 9.26*. To test, hover over any state row in the **State Details** table. Once no state is hovered over, all states are clearly visible (see *Figure 9.27*).

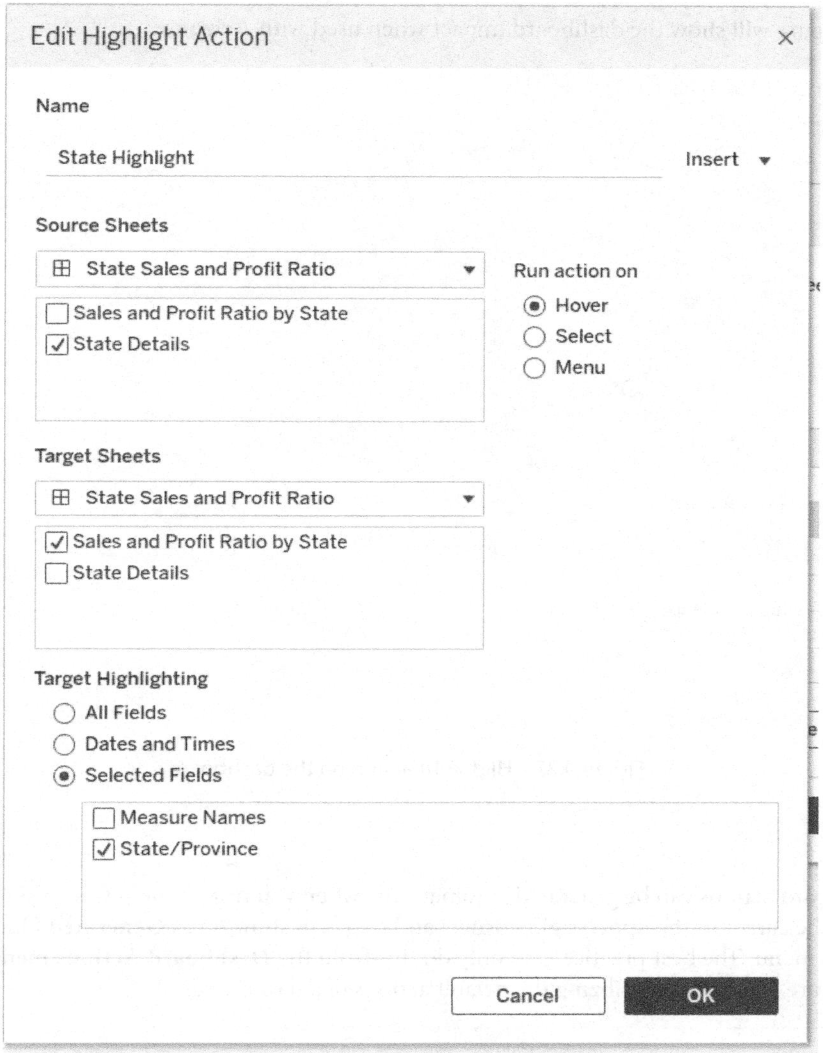

Figure 9.26 – Completed highlight action for State Highlight

The next figure will show the dashboard impact when used with **Arizona**:

State Sales and Profit Ratio

CrossTab

Country/..	State/Province	Sales	Profit Ratio
United	Alabama	$19,511	29.7%
States	Arizona	$35,282	-9.7%
	Arkansas	$11,678	34.3%
	California	$457,688	16.7%

Figure 9.27 – Highlight action on the dashboard

> **Note**
> Dashboard actions can be generated automatically when you trigger them from a sheet menu (from the carrot in the upper-right corner) and they will show up as **Generated** filters in the **Action** menu. The best practice is to only do this from the **Dashboard Actions** menu as you have more control than utilizing the default actions of a dashboard.

Utilizing dashboard actions is important and fun to utilize. However, be careful not to overwhelm the user with actions. Be sure to apply actions that are only useful for insight. Too many actions can also negatively impact the performance of a dashboard. Next, you will learn about the basics of configuring the dashboard layout.

Configuring a dashboard layout

Tableau provides many options by sizing, but also by device, to provide a full experience regardless of how a dashboard is being used. There are so many manipulations that can be applied when considering the layout, but for this examination, only the basics of dashboard options, size options, and fundamental dashboard objects are necessary to know. Learning more about objects, containers, and padding is necessary for real-life applications, but these are not explicitly covered in the examination, so will not be detailed here – however, it's strongly suggested to review this section on Tableau's help page for those elements: `https://help.tableau.com/current/pro/desktop/en-us/dashboards_organize_floatingandtiled.htm#group-items-using-layout-containers`.

In the following section, we will be looking at the options in the **Dashboard** section of a dashboard. Please review *Figure 9.28* for reference:

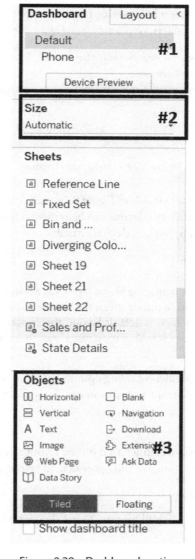

Figure 9.28 – Dashboard section

As you can see in the preceding screenshot, I have highlighted three sections of the **Dashboard** tab. We will be walking through each of these sections in detail in the following sections.

Dashboard options (#1)

Under **Dashboard** on the left side of your dashboard, you see **Default** and **Phone** (these are two standard **Layout** options that Tableau provides you with). Each can be manipulated differently and all, but **Default** setting cannot be removed.

In the **Dashboard** tab in the top menu bar, **Device Layouts** can be accessed, and you can adjust the layouts individually for desktops, tablets, or phones. See *Figure 9.29*:

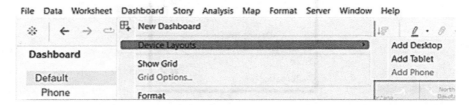

Figure 9.29 – Dashboard Layouts

From the **Dashboard** options menu (left side of *Figure 9.29*), selecting the **Layout** option will show … for **More actions**, and any specific device layout can be removed from here. Default settings cannot be removed but can be overruled by explicit device formats.

> **Note**
> Tableau provides the capability of managing phone layouts as a standard view, but most dashboards are not designed to be used with a phone given the thinner dimension ~375-pixel width of a mobile dashboard. If you only have a default layout, the experience will be similar between devices, except there will be more scrolling for a visualization on a phone instead of a desktop.

Each of the dashboard options has different sizing options based on what works with popular devices. **Device Preview** provides those view options, so you can design for specific user experiences.

Size options (#2)

Users have flexibility with dashboard sizing based on the layout selected. The most flexibility comes from the **Default** layout. In this section, we will cover default layout sizing and defined layout sizing.

Let's begin with default layout sizing.

On the left side of the dashboard, you will find the **Fixed size** option (see *Figure 9.30*):

Figure 9.30 – Fixed size option

Here, you can define the width and height of a dashboard in pixels, and it will not change regardless of the browser you are working from. Tableau defaults to a fixed size and 800-pixel height and 1000-pixel width so most laptops and tablets will not have problems with the view.

Instead of **Fixed size**, you can select **Automatic**, which means the size will automatically adjust based on the screen being viewed from – it is a great feature but can lead to many different visual experiences depending on the screen size and the customary layout of a visual. The other option is to select a range, since users may want more control, and a range defines the minimum and maximum pixels in width and height.

Next, we will check out the defined layout sizing.

Tablets and desktops provide less complex, but generous sizing options to define the sizing for dashboards. Users can select **Default** (which applies the rules of the default sizing layout), **Fit All** (which force-fits the visualizations to the screen to prevent scrolling), or set **Fit Width** (which allows for height adjustment). This is helpful when you have a longer visualization and do not want it to appear *squished* to the user.

Phone layouts are much different. Tableau creates locked custom layouts, which can be unlocked and manipulated. On the phone layout, next to the **More actions** section, there is a lock. Click the *unlock* icon from the phone layout to manipulate the **Default**, **Fit All**, and **Fit Width** options.

Sizing is essential to relate the appropriate experience for users, but you also need to know the basics of objects to help define layouts, as will be covered in the following sections in this chapter.

Objects (#3)

Tableau includes many objects for a dashboard. Each object can be tiled (or applied in a grid on the dashboard), floating (or placed in a specified location not related to the grid layout), or a combination of both tiled and floating elements. The dashboard objects are as follows (from top to bottom, left column followed by right column):

- **Horizontal** – An object that allows other objects/sheets to be stacked left to right
- **Vertical** – An object that stacks objects/sheets from top to bottom
- **Text** – An open text field
- **Image** – A container that is intended to grab an image from your repository or from a web link
- **Web Page** – An embedded object that links to a web file
- **Data Story** – A detailed object that utilizes narrative language to help define the data for users. Although a great Tableau tool, it will not be relevant for the Desktop Specialist exam
- **Blank** – An object that has no contents within and is often used for spacing
- **Navigation** – A button that allows users to navigate between multiple dashboards in a workbook
- **Download** – A button that allows users to download the dashboard in an image, crosstab, PDF, or PowerPoint format
- **Extension** – An object that is external to the Tableau desktop and is utilized to extend the desktop's capabilities. This is another feature that is too advanced for this exam but worth exploring
- **Ask Data** – An advanced Tableau feature that can be utilized in some cases but will provide additional context to data from the mark when applied

The list of objects is extensive. Fortunately, for the exam, you do not need to understand them in detail; you just need to know that some of them exist and can be individually formatted via the **Layout** pane, which I will cover next.

Layout formatting

The Desktop Specialist exam does not dive deeply into formatting individual objects on a dashboard, but it's helpful to understand the basics to better understand one or two questions that may be asked on this topic.

Individual dashboard objects can be modified. Of relevance are vertical and horizontal containers and individual sheets. All can be tiled or floating, and have a border, a background color, outer padding, or inner padding (which could be of equal or unequal pixels per side).

Layout formatting can also be managed when calling on specific layouts. In fact, dashboard objects can be placed in a different layout than the default layout. This means you could stack visualizations left to right or any variety of formats but it will not impact the viewing experience of those who are using a non-specified device (or default). This is particularly helpful when customizing a design for a phone layout versus any other layout. The layout that is best for a desktop (a grid pattern of charts, left to right, and then another row or two of that) will not work for a phone because of its limited width. In that case, charts can be stacked on vertically stacked containers rather than as a vertical stack of horizontal containers.

For more information on layout, you can check out this resource: `https://help.tableau.com/current/pro/desktop/en-us/dashboards_organize_floatingandtiled.htm#group-items-using-layout-containers`. This is worth exploring if you want to start working in development shortly.

Dashboard formatting is covered in the top menu. Select **Dashboard** and **Format**. From there, you can manage the shade or color of the dashboards; the default font, alignment, shading, and border of the dashboard title; the default font and shading of individual worksheet titles; and the font and alignment of text objects. All this formatting can be overridden manually in individual objects.

Formatting is essential for real-world dashboard practitioners to elevate the user experience. The next section will illustrate how to make a story in Tableau (different from **Data Story** in the dashboard objects).

Creating a story and story point

A story is an excellent way to demonstrate using sheets or dashboards to create a visual story in Tableau. You may mention that this is very similar to PowerPoint, but it is also bolstered by the interactive features in Tableau. Creating a story is very simple.

At the bottom right-hand side of the Tableau application (right of individual sheets and dashboards) is the *Story* icon .

In your example, you will be adding the **Sales and Profit by State** and **State Details** sheets and then the **State Sales and Profit Ratio** dashboard to help your users ease into looking at the dashboard. Follow this example to create a basic story:

1. Select the *Story* icon.
2. Rename `Story 1` to `Sales and Profit Ratio by State Story`.
3. Drag **Sales and Profit by State** to the story.
4. Modify the caption block by double-clicking on **Map**.
5. Under **Story** in **New Story Point** on the left side, select **Blank**.
6. Drag **State Details**.
7. Rename that caption `Details`.
8. Repeat *step 5*.
9. Drag **State Sales and Profit Ratio** to that point.
10. Update the caption to `Dashboard`.

11. Select the **Map** story point.

12. Save the workbook.

13. Your story with story points should resemble *Figure 9.31*:

Figure 9.31 – Sales and Profit Ratio by State Story

You have learned the basics of creating, modifying, and preparing individual dashboard and story elements. Next, you will learn how to view and share the data in a workbook.

Viewing and sharing workbook data

Tableau provides a couple of ways to share a workbook for an interactive experience with users or the underlying data as a visual or a table.

Sharing a workbook as a file or on a server

A Tableau desktop file is either a .twb or an XML document that contains all the language of the visualization but contains no external data or images, whereas .twbx is a packaged file that includes the .twb file and the extracted data, images, and other related external files. If you want to share a workbook with a person who has no access to the data, you will have to share a .twbx file. However, a

. twbx file requires extracted data and can be quite large, depending on the size of the data it contains, as it will also contain images and related data.

In a work environment, it is more common to share the workbooks in an on-premises Tableau Server or Tableau-hosted (but site-administered) Tableau Cloud. Although this is a desktop exam, you will require a very basic knowledge of publishing to a server. To publish to a server, you must be authorized as a **Creator** on Tableau Cloud or have project publishing permissions on an on-premises server. To publish to a server, select the **Server** menu item, and then the **Publish Workbook** option. Once accessed, the dialog box will look like *Figure 9.32*:

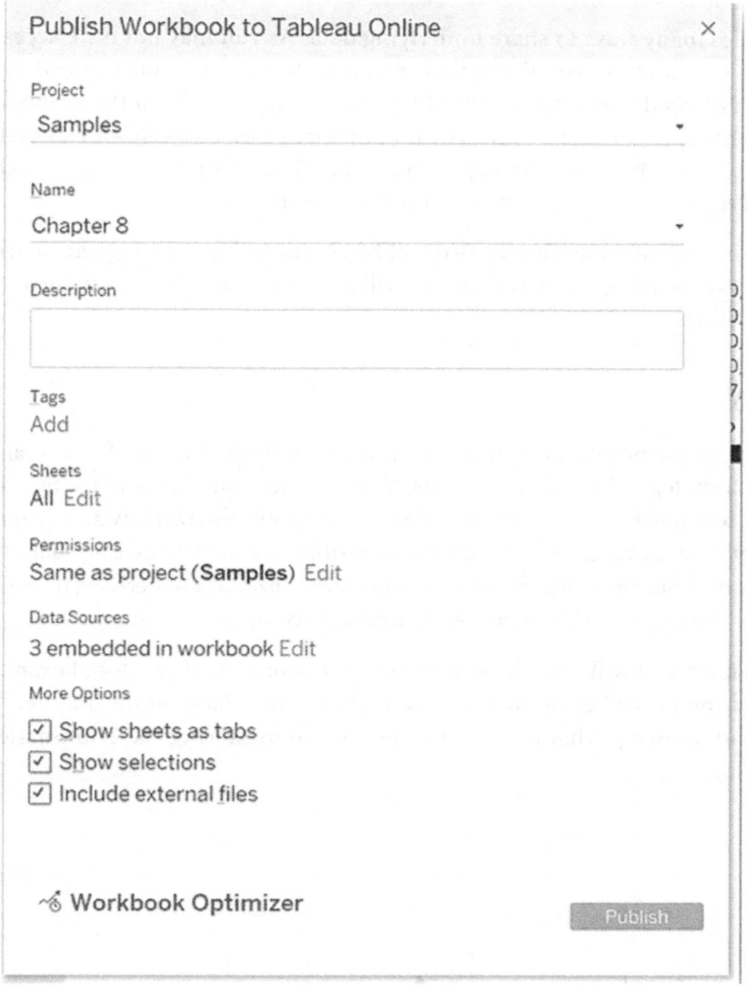

Figure 9.32 – Workbook server publishing dialog box

As you can see from the preceding screenshot, you need to define which project to publish from the dropdown; some projects may be visible but grayed out, which means you have limited publishing rights. You also can name and add a description for the project, add tags to help people find the workbook, show sheets and dashboards or define only the dashboard as visible in the **Sheets** section, define permissions and data source properties (which will not be covered in the exam), or in **More Options**, you can show sheets as individual tabs (on top), show selections made, and include external files (such as images). Once published, these items can also be edited on the server.

View and export underlying data

Tableau provides many ways to share underlying data. As you may not have access to a server or workbook, the best way to share the options you have for sharing underlying data is by directing you to Tableau's *Help* document for publishing data (as it covers both the dashboard application and server) at `https://help.tableau.com/current/reader/desktop/en-us/reader_publish.htm`, and for exporting as a PDF at `https://help.tableau.com/current/reader/desktop/en-us/reader_export.htm`.

Although no more than a question or two will be committed to viewing and sharing data on the examination, understanding the core concepts will help you and your users tremendously in relating Tableau's capabilities.

Summary

In this chapter, you learned how to finetune your charts and tables with color, size, and shapes, while manipulating font, legends, and animations. You enhanced this knowledge by creating a simple dashboard and learning how to format basic dashboards, apply interactivity and actions, and format a dashboard for various devices. These functions are further extended by sharing your visualizations as a file, on a server or cloud environment, or by sharing a visualizations underlying data. Congratulations, you have completed all the Tableau pre-work needed to complete the examination.

In the next chapter, you will learn how to prepare for your virtual proctored exam. The proctored exam is a closely monitored environment without the use of Tableau or the internet. Without proper preparation and knowing what to expect, your path to mastering the examination becomes far more challenging.

Knowledge check

To check your knowledge of this chapter, here are a few questions that this chapter's material will help you answer. The questions that have been selected aren't intended to trick you but to provide you with a learning benchmark to give you a foundational understanding to help prepare you for the exam. The answers are marked in italics:

1. Which items are correct about dashboard filters? (Select all that apply.)

    A. *Added to one sheet but not visible on a dashboard*

    B. *Added as a dashboard filter and change the items in multiple sheets*

    C. *Added as a dashboard action that can be defined on all or selected fields*

    D. Added to a dashboard as a highlighter action

2. Which item cannot be specifically attributed as a legend type?

    A. Shape

    B. *Value*

    C. Size

    D. Color

3. What is the correct response for how devices can override a default layout specification?

    A. *Desktops, tablets, and phones can be specified to override the default specifications*

    B. Desktops and tablets can override the default, but phones cannot

    C. If a default layout is used, then no other device layout can override that layout

    D. Deleting a default layout will enable all other layouts to be customizable

Part 3: The Final Prep

You have all the knowledge required to work with Tableau and master the Desktop Certification from *Part 1* and *Part 2*, but *Part 3* is where you will prepare further and test your understanding.

The final part consists of two chapters. The first chapter contains all the information you need to get ready for a proctored exam with a focus on the online proctored environment. The second chapter provides a mock examination in a similar style with similar weighting to the actual examination and similar questions.

By the end of this section, you will see whether you are ready and which chapters require your attention. You will also have no surprises come exam day, which will undoubtedly provide you with the opportunity to get the best score possible.

Combined with the learning from prior parts, you will have gained preparedness, practical knowledge, and an understanding of the essential domains so that you can not only take the test but also begin to work with Tableau Desktop in a professional setting.

This part comprises the following chapters:

- *Chapter 10, Exam Preparation*
- *Chapter 11, Mock Test*

Exam Preparation

This chapter will be much different from the previous chapters. In this chapter, we will focus on being best prepared for the examination to score as high as possible or increase the likelihood of scoring well. Having a knowledge-based exam without the use of the Tableau application and internet while being actively monitored adds levels of complexities that need to be prepared for. Since most people will not take this examination in person, this preparation coverage is focused on the online proctored environment.

In this chapter, we will cover the following topics:

- What you need to have prepared before scheduling the examination
- Last-minute preparation
- How to prepare yourself for success when taking a proctored exam (with a focus on online testing)

Technical requirements

The only technical requirement for this examination is a computer with dependable internet access.

Preparation through examination scheduling

A knowledge-based exam for Tableau means that there are questions in the test intended to certify your understanding of the tool without being able to use Tableau. This is very difficult as Tableau is a tool that people utilize with hands-on experience; terms and how processes are done are second nature and not strongly considered by most practitioners. In addition, Tableau expects you to have 3-6 months of daily and consistent use of the tool to be ready for the examination. This book crams that knowledge and applies a combination of academic and practical knowledge to prepare you even better for the examination in far less time.

The following sections will help you determine system needs, how to access the examination site, and what to do once you are there to schedule your exam.

Examination basics

The time to take the exam is 60 minutes. The question format is multiple choice (e.g. select a single response from four or five options) or multiple responses (generally selecting two or three answers from four or five options). There are 45 questions, of which 40 are scored (this means five questions are unscored, but it is not clear which questions those are). Passing is 750 marks out of a possible 1,000 – the scoring is scaled, which means some questions have more weight. As of December 2022, the only languages offered for the exam are English, Japanese, and Simplified Chinese.

Preparing for the online examination before the day of the exam

I want you to be set up for success. Before you even schedule the examination, confirm, or get access to the following items. Here is a checklist of things to review and be comfortable with before you schedule the examination:

- Computer/Mac needs:

  - A desktop or laptop computer. Phones (outside of check-in) and most tablets will not be permitted.

  - An operating system using Windows 10 (64-bit), or at least a macOS of 10.15 and above.

  - At least 4 GB of RAM.

  - Minimum resolution of 1024 * 768 and 16-bit color.

  - Internet connection of at least 6 Mbps download and 3 Mbps upload (however, I would not feel comfortable under 20 Mbps for download and 6 Mbps upload).

  - Webcam with a minimum of 640 x 480/10 fps resolution.

  - Computer with audio speakers and microphone (wired or Bluetooth setups will likely not be approved).

Most of the preceding features can be viewed by looking at your computer properties and newer full-size laptops or desktops meet these conditions.

- Other considerations are as follows:

  - The computer should not be a work computer as many of these have firewalls that may prevent the test from functioning on the computer.

  - Have a space to access with little or no interruption. This is important as it will not only negatively impact your ability to focus on the examination, but you may also be interrupted by the proctor as they verify you are taking the exam appropriately.

If the preceding items cannot be fulfilled, you can consider taking the test in person as there are thousands of testing facilities and you will be able to select that option when scheduling the examination.

Scheduling the examination and additional preparation

You may be able to schedule your examination for the same day as you take your exam, but I would encourage you not to do it that way. You can cancel and reschedule your examination if it is more than 48 hours away. You also want to make sure you are taking the exam on a day with little to no interruption.

Here are the steps to access the examination page and schedule your examination:

1. Go to `https://home.pearsonvue.com/tableau`.

2. Select the **Log-in** button (currently on the upper right-hand corner) to create an account for testing.

3. Once the account is created, you will be able to access a dashboard similar to what you see in *Figure 10.1*.

4. Select **Schedule My Exam**, as seen here:

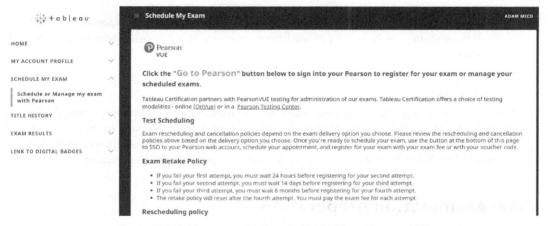

Figure 10.1: Tableau examination dashboard from Pearson VUE

5. Simply read the notes and select the **GO TO PEARSON** button at the bottom.

6. From here, bookmark this dashboard, as seen in *Figure 10.2*, for ease of access.

7. Then you will need to select the **TDS-C01: Tableau Desktop Specialist** exam, as seen in *Figure 10.2*:

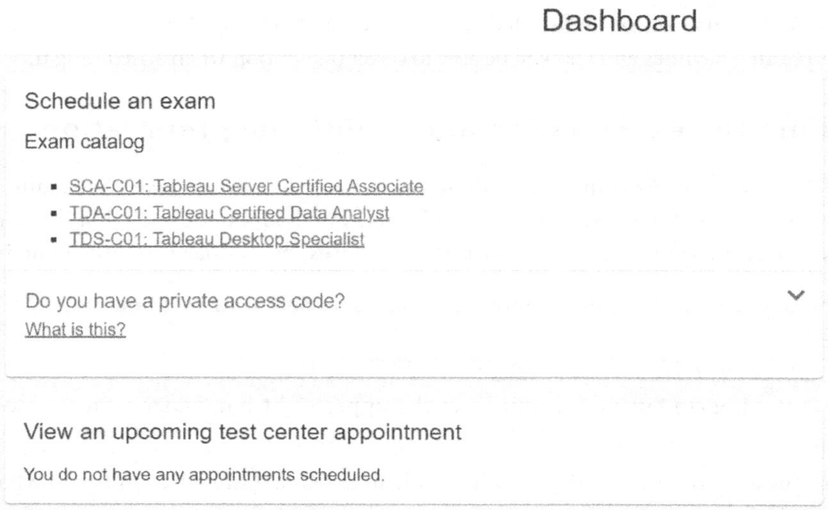

Dashboard

Schedule an exam

Exam catalog

- SCA-C01: Tableau Server Certified Associate
- TDA-C01: Tableau Certified Data Analyst
- TDS-C01: Tableau Desktop Specialist

Do you have a private access code?   ⌄
What is this?

View an upcoming test center appointment

You do not have any appointments scheduled.

Figure 10.2: Pearson Tableau exam dashboard

8. Follow their guided steps to schedule your exam (note: both online and in-person are scheduled from the website – make sure to please have your payment information accessible as the cost is $100).

> **Scheduling tip**
>
> Think of a time of day when you are at your peak capacity. We all have ups and downs during the day as far as our function is concerned, so if you have a better function in the afternoon, schedule during that period. Also, consider a couple of hours for a last-minute cram and an additional 30 minutes to make sure your environment is good for the examination.

Final examination preparation

Once the examination is scheduled, you really need to make sure you cover any knowledge gaps and do enough to make sure you get more points as that may be the difference in whether the certification is attained.

Post-scheduling preparation

Here are my suggestions for preparation:

- Run the system test and exam simulation as soon as possible (which will be sent once the online exam is scheduled).

- Do a quick scan of *Chapters 1-8* and dive deeper into topics that were more challenging for you.

- Create flashcards of some of the terminology. A good free site for this is quizlet.com.

- Prepare your environment for your test as early as possible – work on it as much as possible before the exam to increase your comfort level.

- Take your mock exams (or retake) in *Chapter 12, Mock Tests*, in your new environment, and only use one monitor for the second half of it to resemble more closely what the actual test environment will be.

- When taking the mock exam, have your place clear and remove your phone, anything with Bluetooth, or any artificial noise so the proctored experience will closely resemble the actual experience.

- If you are prone to test anxiety, do not try to cram everything the day before the exam; in a perfect world, do not study the night prior to the and get a proper night's rest.

The prior tips are what I use for online proctored exams to ensure I get the best out of my experience during the examination. The right amount of preparation allowed me to be at peak or near peak capacity while testing. Even taking this exam, given my vast experience with Tableau, I was very nervous because I had never taken a proctored exam online. Next, we will discuss what to do on the day of the examination.

Exam day preparation

Exam day is always stressful, but hopefully, your preparation helped reduce that stress. Here are my suggestions for exam day:

- Block at least 4 hours, but preferably the entire day.

- At least 2.5 hours before the exam, study for 2 hours. I would spend 1 hour studying the mock examination and then 1 more hour on terms or concepts.

- You will get a notification from Pearson VUE between 15 and 30 minutes before the test, so even before the final test practice, make sure your area is properly set up, and have your government-issued photo ID and phone accessible – not being prepared for this will cause more stress at the start of the test.

- Make sure to breathe well and calmly immediately before and during the exam—focus on your breathing.

- When taking the test, someone will be monitoring sound and your movement. You may be questioned when there is a foreign sound, when looking away from the monitor, or even talking to yourself. Remind yourself to look directly at your monitor.

- Remember to read the questions thoroughly and all options before you attempt to form an answer.

- You have a little over a minute per question – a tip that has worked for me is to go through the test once and answer the easy questions. Answering those questions helps build your confidence and then you can go back and answer the more complex questions.

- As time permits, go back and review your answers. If given the full hour, use that full hour. Of course, you may second-guess yourself and choose and incorrect answer once or twice but understanding a question and answering that understood question outweighs the cost of second-guessing.

Once the examination is done

Within minutes of submitting the examination, you will learn whether you passed and what your final score was. In addition, if you pass, you will get a Credly certification for the examination, much like the one I shared in *Chapter 1*. Either way, try to give yourself a minute to absorb the result.

Once you get the Credly certification, I strongly encourage you to share on LinkedIn and publish it to your profile. Anyone with access to that Credly link will be able to see you earned that badge. As mentioned previously, unlike other Tableau certifications, this is a lifetime certification. Please be sure to tag me and share this book on social media if you feel it helped you earn your credential.

If you did not pass the examination, please take the test again at your next convenience. You have experience with the questions and will have a better idea of what your focus should be – although this book is designed to help you pass most efficiently on attempt one, you may need to sort out some of the core concepts represented in *Chapters 1-8*.

Summary

In this chapter, you learned what you needed to validate before scheduling the examination, how and where to schedule the exam, how to prepare between scheduling and exam day, exam day preparation, and what you can do after.

In the next chapter, you will have the opportunity to work on two mock tests. One focuses on more practical knowledge based on a visualization developed for that exam, but the other applies more of the structure you will see on the actual examination with the wording, questions, and answers. Both will challenge you in different ways and will prepare you for the examination itself.

Mock Test

This is the chapter that you have prepared for. This is an incredible way to verify your learning or help you know what to focus on before taking the test. The following questions are not on the examination but will align with their scoring weights. You should take the examination multiple times to verify your understanding and whether it's consistent. The other thing is that the exam will be scored to 1,000 and each question will be valued at 25 points. You need to score 750 points to pass (answer 30 questions correctly).

Although Tableau's weight detail on each question is proprietary, we can get very close based on their preparation guide here: https://mkt.tableau.com/files/TableauDesktopSpecialist_ExamGuide.pdf. For our training purposes, you will have 10 questions on **Connecting to and Preparing Data (CPD)**, 10 on **Sharing Insights (SI)**, 14 on **Exploring and Analyzing Data (EAD)**, and 6 on **Understanding Tableau Concepts (UTC)**, with no unscored questions.

Since Tableau's exam includes 45 questions (5 unscored) and a 60-minute time limit, you should prorate the time to take the mock examination to 53 minutes, given the 5-question reduction.

Technical requirements

The only technical requirement for this examination is a computer with dependable internet access. Using Tableau for the mock exam is acceptable for a first or second run through, but you will be best prepared by not using the tool when taking the examination.

Mock exam

This is a 40-question mock exam. I will include domain initials next to each question to provide insight (as you will see), but Tableau does not include that information in their examinations.

Those domains are as follows:

- CPD
- SI

- EAD

- UTC

Remember that you have 53 minutes for this examination, so try to take them without using Google or Tableau, as you will not have access to them during the examination. Please set a timer for 53 minutes, and stop answering the questions when you reach that time.

The answers are shown after the test on *page 15*.

Start the exam

Question 1: Which of the following is not a data type in Tableau?

    A. Date

    B. Numeric

    C. Polygon

    D. Date and time

Question 2: In the Tableau Order of Operations, please select all true statements from the following options:

    A. Extract filters are the first query Tableau applies when considering filters.

    B. Fixed **LODs** (or **level of detail** calculations) can be impacted by dimension filters.

    C. Measure filters impact trend lines.

    D. Table calc filters are the second-to-last filters referenced in the Order of Operations.

Question 3: Which chart type is used frequently to track changes over time using a continuous date field?

    A. A point map

    B. A highlight table

    C. A bar chart

    D. A line chart

Question 4: On the data source pane, which option is inaccurate?

    A. Tableau will pull in a table if you have at least one data source connected.

    B. When at least one table brings in the data, a data source filter can be added.

    C. You can create a union with another table.

    D. None. All are accurate.

Question 5: Which data type is required to build a histogram chart?

    A.   String

    B.   Geography

    C.   Bin

    D.   Numeric

    E.   Boolean

Question 6: For viz animations, how can animations be manipulated in Tableau? (Select all that apply.)

    A.   Make viz animations simultaneous.

    B.   Change the speed of the animation.

    C.   Choose specific marks on a chart to animate.

    D.   Create an animation action in Dashboard Actions.

Question 7: Which file type is used for a packaged Tableau workbook?

    A.   `.hyper`

    B.   `.twb`

    C.   `.tds`

    D.   `.twbx`

Question 8: A _____ is when you are combining tables to append to them because they have the same fields or columns:

    A.   Join

    B.   Union

    C.   Relationship

    D.   Calculation

Question 9: When considering groups and sets, select all the following options that apply to both:

    A.   They can be referenced in calculations.

    B.   They can be used in dashboard actions.

    C.   They are based on dimensions from other fields.

    D.   They have their own unique data type icons.

Question 10: When working with text in Tableau, which options can be modified in the desktop application? (Select all that apply.)

    A.   Spell check

    B.   Font size

    C.   Justify alignment

    D.   Text color

Question 11: Which field, when brought into view in Tableau, will create an axis rather than a header?

    A.   Continuous

    B.   Numeric

    C.   String

    D.   Discrete

Question 12: When creating a relationship in Tableau, a _____ field is required to relate the tables:

    A.   Geographic

    B.   String

    C.   Common

    D.   Dimensional

Question 13: When would you use COUNTD over the COUNT function in Tableau? (Select all that apply.)

    A.   To see the row count

    B.   To get a distinct count of a dimension appearing in data

    C.   To omit duplicate counts of a dimension, due to bad data or data densification

    D.   To make a data range filter

Question 14: At the worksheet level, where can a font be formatted?

    A.   Worksheet titles

    B.   Totals

    C.   Headers

    D.   Tooltips

    E.   All of the above

Question 15: How can you save a data source as an extract?

A. You do nothing; Tableau saves your data source as an extract automatically.

B. Create a calculated field using the EXTRACT function.

C. You cannot extract a data source.

D. Select **Extract** from the data source pane and follow the prompts.

Question 16: Select all that are true about continuous fields:

A. Their pills are colored green in Tableau.

B. When applied to a color mark, they result in a selection of sequential or diverging colors.

C. They contain only string data.

D. They require a parameter to work.

Question 17: A _____ value is defined by the absence of data:

A. Null

B. Dynamic

C. Total

D. Incremental

Question 18: A dashboard layout can be defined for which of the following devices? (Select all that apply.)

A. Desktop

B. Tablet

C. Laptop

D. Phone

Question 19: Tableau adds _____ and _____ on rows and columns when a geographic field is added as a detail to the **Marks** section to create a map:

A. Minimum and maximum

B. Latitude and longitude

C. States and countries

D. Maps and map plots

Question 20: When editing a tooltip, what can you not do with it?

    A.   Create it as its own worksheet

    B.   Insert a sheet

    C.   Edit a font

    D.   Add a field to dynamically modify its text

Question 21: What is true about creating or editing a calculated field?

    A.   A parameter is no different than a calculated field.

    B.   A calculated field will be identified by an equal sign before the data type icon.

    C.   Tableau will prompt you in the editor if a calculation is invalid.

    D.   A calculated field cannot perform logical functions.

Question 22: When changing the number format, which of the following changes can you make? (Select all that apply.)

    A.   Make a whole number

    B.   A change to a dynamic fraction

    C.   A change to currency

    D.   A change to a string or text data

Question 23: When creating a _____, you define subordinate fields:

    A.   Discrete measure

    B.   Continuous measure

    C.   Hierarchy

    D.   Set

Question 24: How do you access a shape mark?

    A.   It appears automatically.

    B.   Select **Shape** from the **Marks** dropdown.

    C.   You must bring a measure in as a dimension.

    D.   You need to add a shape data type as a detail of the **Marks** section.

Question 25: A measure must be based on a _____ data type:

    A.   Numerical

    B.   Boolean

    C.   Cluster

    D.   Text

Question 26: Select the applicable false statements about common chart types in Tableau:

    A.   A stacked bar chart is a bar chart segmented by dimensions.

    B.   A combined axis chart has one axis whereas a dual axis chart has two axes.

    C.   A highlight table is the same as a table but includes a shape and color to provide additional insight.

    D.   A bar chart is based on the creation of an axis whereas a line chart is based on the use of a header.

Question 27: A _____ can be added to a sheet (or dashboard) and is only available if the sheet has a size, shape, or color mark:

    A.   Highlight

    B.   Label

    C.   Legend

    D.   Parameter

Question 28: What happens to a union if a column is added that is not part of another table?

    A.   The column will be added but with a null value in any row of the table(s) without that column.

    B.   Tableau will not allow a union and bring up an error.

    C.   The union can still be made, but it excludes any tables with mismatched fields.

    D.   None of the above.

Question 29: Select all true options that apply to a discrete dimension:

    A.   A discrete dimension can be used to create a header.

    B.   A discrete dimension can be a date field.

    C.   In some situations, a numerical data type can be a discrete dimension and not a discrete or continuous measure.

    D.   A discrete geographical field can be used to trigger Tableau's map features.

Question 30: A _____ date filter can create a filter showing a date (anchored or not anchored), using day(s), week(s), month(s), quarter(s), or year(s):

A. Calculated

B. Range

C. Relative

D. Special

Question 31: Select the best option for a default Tableau dashboard layout:

A. The dimensions are 1,000 pixels wide and 800 pixels tall.

B. With a phone layout.

C. At a fixed size.

D. All of the above.

Question 32: On the data source pane, an option called the data _____ can be used to look at data and clean it for analysis in Tableau:

A. Interpreter

B. Relationship

C. Fixer

D. Action

Question 33: A common example of a _____ set is to have a condition to show values in and out of the set:

A. Fixed

B. Hierarchical

C. Dynamic

D. Relative

Question 34: Which functions are not considered string functions?

A. MIN

B. MAKELINE

C. ABS

D. TRIM

Question 35: What is true when you add a dimension to a view?

    A.   It changes the level of aggregation.

    B.   It does not get impacted by a Context filter.

    C.   It will never impact a table calculation.

    D.   Among other additions, it can be added to a row, column, or mark.

Question 36: What is true about a URL action in Tableau? (Select all that apply.)

    A.   A static website can only be used for a URL action.

    B.   A URL action can modify an object in the dashboard or a new browser tab.

    C.   A field value can be used to make a URL action dynamic.

    D.   A URL action can only be applied by a selection.

Question 37: If a table contains joins on the data source pains, those joins can be seen by double-clicking on a table in the _____ layer.

    A.   Logical

    B.   Physical

    C.   Union

    D.   Data

Question 38: What is true about categorical color marks? (Select all that apply.)

    A.   You can change the opacity of colors.

    B.   You can select advanced options.

    C.   You can select colors for each dimension.

    D.   You can select a diverging color palette.

Question 39: What will happen to a field with a thousand rows when it comes into Tableau with 800 dates, 199 blanks (null), and 1 result of *N/A*?

    A.   It becomes a date field because most of the results are dates.

    B.   It becomes an errored field because Tableau cannot accept blank values.

    C.   It becomes an errored field because Tableau cannot figure out what to do with three data types (date, nulls, and strings).

    D.   It becomes a string field because of the single *N/A*. Tableau would have otherwise made it a date field.

Question 40: What can you not modify when working with background layers in maps?

    A.   The map style

    B.   The size of the dimension(s) in a map

    C.   The amount of *washout* a map has

    D.   Background map layers

Congratulations! You have finished the mock examination. The next section covers the answers to the mock examination and points out the exam domain it covers.

Exam answers

The following section will show the question number and answer(s) (on the first line) and the exam domain of the question, plus the chapter numbers in which the domain was covered:

- Question 1 | C:

  The domain covered was *Domain 2, Exploring and Analyzing Data*, and this area is focused on in *Chapters 1, 3, 4, 5, 7,* and *8*.

- Question 2 | A:

  The domain covered was *Domain 4, Understanding Tableau Concepts*, and this area is focused on in *Chapters 1* and *4*.

- Question 3 | D:

  The domain covered was *Domain 2, Exploring and Analyzing Data*, and this area is focused on in *Chapters 1, 3, 4, 5, 7,* and *8*.

- Question 4 | A:

  The domain covered was *Domain 1, Connecting to and Preparing Data*, and this area is focused on in *Chapters 2* and *6*.

- Question 5 | C:

  The domain covered was *Domain 2, Exploring and Analyzing Data*, and this area is focused on in *Chapters 1, 3, 4, 5, 7,* and *8*.

- Question 6 | A and B:

  The domain covered was *Domain 3, Sharing Insights*, and this area is focused on in *Chapters 3, 4, 5,* and *9*.

- Question 7 | D:

  The domain covered was *Domain 3, Sharing Insights*, and this area is focused on in *Chapters 3, 4, 5,* and *9*.

- Question 8 | B:

  The domain covered was *Domain 1, Connecting to and Preparing Data*, and this area is focused on in *Chapters 2* and *6*.

- Question 9 | A, B, and C:

  The domain covered was *Domain 2, Exploring and Analyzing Data*, and this area is focused on in *Chapters 1, 3, 4, 5, 7,* and *8*.

- Question 10 | B and D:

  The domain covered was *Domain 3, Sharing Insights*, and this area is focused on in *Chapters 3, 4, 5,* and *9*.

- Question 11 | A:

  The domain covered was *Domain 4, Understanding Tableau Concepts*, and this area is focused on in *Chapters 1* and *4*.

- Question 12 | C:

  The domain covered was *Domain 1, Connecting to and Preparing Data*, and this area is focused on in *Chapters 2* and *6*.

- Question 13 | B and C:

  The domain covered was *Domain 2, Exploring and Analyzing Data*, and this area is focused on in *Chapters 1, 3, 4, 5, 7,* and *8*.

- Question 14 | E:

  The domain covered was *Domain 3, Sharing Insights*, and this area is focused on in *Chapters 3, 4, 5,* and *9*.

- Question 15 | D:

  The domain covered was *Domain 1, Connecting to and Preparing Data*, and this area is focused on in *Chapters 2* and *6*.

- Question 16 | A and B:

  The domain covered was *Domain 4, Understanding Tableau Concepts*, and this area is focused on in *Chapters 1* and *4*.

- Question 17 | A:

  The domain covered was *Domain 2, Exploring and Analyzing Data*, and this area is focused on in *Chapters 1, 3, 4, 5, 7,* and *8*.

- Question 18 | A, B, and D:

  The domain covered was *Domain 2, Exploring and Analyzing Data*, and this area is focused on in *Chapters 1, 3, 4, 5, 7*, and *8*.

- Question 19 | B:

  The domain covered was *Domain 1, Connecting to and Preparing Data*, and this area is focused on in *Chapters 2* and *6*.

- Question 20 | A:

  The domain covered was *Domain 3, Sharing Insights*, and this area is focused on in *Chapters 3, 4, 5*, and *9*.

- Question 21 | B and C:

  The domain covered was *Domain 2, Exploring and Analyzing Data*, and this area is focused on in *Chapters 1, 3, 4, 5, 7*, and *8*.

- Question 22 | A and C:

  The domain covered was *Domain 1, Connecting to and Preparing Data*, and this area is focused on in *Chapters 2* and *6*.

- Question 23 | C:

  The domain covered was *Domain 2, Exploring and Analyzing Data*, and this area is focused on in *Chapters 1, 3, 4, 5, 7*, and *8*.

- Question 24 | B:

  The domain covered was *Domain 3, Sharing Insights*, and this area is focused on in *Chapters 3, 4, 5*, and *9*.

- Question 25 | A:

  The domain covered was *Domain 4, Understanding Tableau Concepts*, and this area is focused on in *Chapters 1* and *4*.

- Question 26 | B and D:

  The domain covered was *Domain 2, Exploring and Analyzing Data*, and this area is focused on in *Chapters 1, 3, 4, 5, 7*, and *8*.

- Question 27 | C:

  The domain covered was *Domain 3, Sharing Insights*, and this area is focused on in *Chapters 3, 4, 5*, and *9*.

- Question 28 | B:

  The domain covered was *Domain 1, Connecting to and Preparing Data*, and this area is focused on in *Chapters 2* and *6*.

- Question 29 | A and B:

  The domain covered was *Domain 4, Understanding Tableau Concepts*, and this area is focused on in *Chapters 1* and *4*.

- Question 30 | C:

  The domain covered was *Domain 2, Exploring and Analyzing Data*, and this area is focused on in *Chapters 1, 3, 4, 5, 7*, and *8*.

- Question 31 | D:

  The domain covered was *Domain 3, Sharing Insights*, and this area is focused on in *Chapters 3, 4, 5*, and *9*.

- Question 32 | D:

  The domain covered was *Domain 1, Connecting to and Preparing Data*, and this area is focused on in *Chapters 2* and *6*.

- Question 33 | C:

  The domain covered was *Domain 2, Exploring and Analyzing Data*, and this area is focused on in *Chapters 1, 3, 4, 5, 7*, and *8*.

  Question 34 | B and C:

  The domain covered was *Domain 2, Exploring and Analyzing Data*, and this area is focused on in *Chapters 1, 3, 4, 5, 7*, and *8*.

- Question 35 | A and D:

  The domain covered was *Domain 4, Understanding Tableau Concepts*, and this area is focused on in *Chapters 1* and *4*.

- Question 36 | B and C:

  The domain covered was *Domain 3, Sharing Insights*, and this area is focused on in *Chapters 3, 4, 5*, and *9*.

- Question 37 | B:

  The domain covered was *Domain 1, Connecting to and Preparing Data*, and this area is focused on in *Chapters 2* and *6*.

- Question 38 | A and C:

  The domain covered was *Domain 3, Sharing Insights*, and this area is focused on in *Chapters 3, 4, 5,* and *9*.

- Question 39 | D:

  The domain covered was *Domain 1, Connecting to and Preparing Data*, and this area is focused on in *Chapters 2* and *6*.

- Question 40 | B:

  The domain covered was *Domain 2, Exploring and Analyzing Data*, and this area is focused on in *Chapters 1, 3, 4, 5, 7,* and *8*.

Now that you can see what the correct answers to the examination are, what does that mean for you, and how do you score it? The next section will cover scoring for the entire examination and individual domains.

Exam scoring

I want you to get the most out of this book and your preparation. You will need to really invest time in the critical scoring element. The following sections will cover basic scoring and domain scoring to help you really understand where to invest more time for better understanding and preparation. Also, consider the time it took to complete the examination. If you could not complete the exam in 53 minutes, consider the questions and domains that gave you problems and study those chapters further.

Basic scoring

Each question is worth 25 points, which comes out to a total of 1,000 points for the total exam. To get 25 points, you need to get the entirety of the answer correct. This is difficult for multiple-choice questions, but all the correct selections must be made – there is no partial credit for having one correct answer to a two-part question. For example, if the answer is A, C, and D, *25* points is only scored if all selections were made – any other combination results in a score of *0* for that question. In short, a question score can either be *0* or *25*.

For the full examination, if you answered 30 questions correctly, you earn 750 points. This is the lowest passing mark. If you answered fewer than 30 questions correctly, you would not earn enough points to pass the mock examination.

The next piece is a domain breakdown. This is to help you further study and determine stronger versus weaker domains. I highly recommend digging further into domain scoring to really understand how you scored.

Domain scoring

This subsection is to help you understating your scoring, based on each domain covered in the book, as follows:

- *Domain 1, Connecting to and Preparing Data*, is covered in *Chapters 2* and *6* in the book. The following questions were related to that section: *4, 8, 12, 15, 19, 22, 28, 32, 37*, and *39*. You need to answer 8 of 10 correctly to pass this domain.

- *Domain 2, Exploring and Analyzing Data*, is covered in *Chapters 1, 3, 4, 5, 7*, and *8* in the book. The following questions were related to that section: *1, 3, 5, 9, 13, 17, 18, 21, 23, 26, 30, 33, 34*, and *40*. You need to answer 11 of 14 correctly to pass this domain.

- *Domain 3, Connecting to and Preparing Data*, is covered in *Chapters 3, 4, 5*, and *9* in the book. The following questions were related to that section: *6, 7, 10, 14, 20, 24, 27, 31, 36*, and *38*. You need to answer 8 of 10 correctly to pass this domain.

- *Domain 4, Understanding Tableau Concepts*, is covered in *Chapters 1* and *4* in the book. The following questions were related to that section: *2, 11, 16, 25, 29*, and *35*. You need to answer 5 of 6 correctly to pass this domain.

Note that you will need to answer at least 32 questions correctly to pass all domains because none of them divide equally to 75%. I also did not give you the specific place in the book to look up the results of each question – the reason for this is that the questions will not be the same as the examination, and you would be best served by studying the breadth of content, especially if you are not grasping a domain.

What's next?

This mock examination was intentionally difficult. It is gauging your understanding of the concepts beyond what is on the page, based on your work with the tool. Passing the examination and all domains will ensure that you have the tools to ace the Tableau exam.

Not passing the examination on the first or second time is not something that should discourage you. If you have time, do not retest for at least a couple of days to help lose those answers from your short-term memory. Use that time to refocus on the chapters covered in each domain that you need to work on, and also make sure to cover the hands-on exercises.

Even if you do pass the mock examination, please remember to continue to cover key areas in the period between the mock exam and the real one to to help retain your knowledge. Furthermore, I encourage you to practice on your own.

The best way to improve your skills quickly after this book and other related Packt books is by joining the Tableau community here: `https://www.tableau.com/blog/ways-get-started-tableau-community`.

The Tableau community is not only a social media active group of data fanatics, but they also provide an extensive amount of free resources, including user forums, blogs, video and blog tutorials, networking events, themed data visualization initiatives, user groups (virtual and in-person), and so much more (and it's mostly free).

Summary

In this chapter, you took an exam, with scoring weights modeled after the actual exam. You evaluated your strengths and weaknesses and determined where to commit additional studying resources.

Thank you so much for reading and actively engaging in the content. Please let me know how you did on LinkedIn (`https://www.linkedin.com/in/adammico/`) or Twitter (`https://twitter.com/AdamMico1`). Please leave a review on Amazon or whatever outlet you purchased this book from.

Index

A

aggregate functions 82
AVG 82
COUNT 82
COUNTD 82
MAX 82
MIN 82
reference link 82
SUM 82
analytics
applying, at worksheet level 162
area charts 134
creating 134, 135
insights 136

B

bar chart 120
generating 121, 122
bins 171
creating 171, 172
visualization example 173
blue field
versus green field 69-72

C

calculations 78
building 84-86
calculated field, creating 83, 84
creating 83
categorical color marks 176-178
management 179
chart
formatting 38-45
color marks
categorical color marks 176-178
managing 179
quantitative color marks 178, 179
using 176
column chart 120
computed sorting 162
Consumer header 37
continuous dimension
versus discrete dimension 69-72
Creator 219
crosstabs 122, 123

D

dashboard 196
creating 196
modifying 196
modifying, with filter action 208-210
modifying, with highlight action 210-212
dashboard actions 207
adding 202, 203
filter actions 203, 204
highlight actions 205, 206
URL actions 206, 207
dashboard layout
configuring 212-214
dashboard options (#1) 214
formatting 216
objects (#3) 216
size options (#2) 214, 215
dashboard pre-work 196-198
actions, adding 202, 203
dashboard layout, configuring 212-214
interactive elements, adding 200-202
worksheets, adding 199
data connection 25-27
data dimensions
Boolean or true/false fields 67
calculated field 68
date 67
geographic 67
groups 67
hierarchies 67
string dimensions 67
working with 66, 67
data measures 68, 69
data model
creating 105-108
data, organizing 152
data grouping 152
grouping data exercise 152-154

groups, editing 155
hierarchies, creating 155, 156
hierarchy, editing 156
hierarchy exercise, creating 156
sets, working with 157
data properties
managing 108-112
Data Source pane
data cleaning functionalities 31-33
extract, creating from 98-101
fields, formatting 29-31
overview 27-29
data structure
basics 22
data categorization 23
data cleanliness basics 24
data columns/fields 23
data granularity 23
data rows 23
data types 23
data visualization 25
format 22, 23
pivoted data, versus unpivoted data 24
data visualization 21
chart formatting 38-45
one-chart data visualization 36-38
tooltips 56-63
date functions 80
DATEDIFF 80
DATETRUNC 80
MAX 80
MIN 80
reference link 80
TODAY 80
density maps 147
building 148
use cases 148
discrete dimension
versus continuous dimension 69-72

diverging color marks 178

dual-axis chart 140
  creating 140
  insights 141

dynamic sets 160
  creating 160
  visualization, creating 161, 162

dynamic sorting
  creating 163, 164

E

exam preparation
  exam day preparation 229
  examination basics 226
  examination, scheduling 227, 228
  final preparation 228
  online examination 226
  post examination 230
  post-scheduling preparation 228
  through examination scheduling 225

extracted data connection
  creating 98
  creating, from sheet 101-105

F

field labels formatting
  reference link 42

field sort 162

filled maps 143
  creating 143
  insights 144

filters and actions 46-55

fixed sets 157
  creating 157, 158
  visualization, creating 159

fonts
  alignment options 184
  configuring 181
  formatting, at workbook level 181, 182
  formatting, at worksheet level 182
  formatting, in Tooltip 185-187
  formatting notes 187, 188
  formatting options 182, 183

functions. *See* **Tableau functions**

fundamental charts
  area charts 134, 135
  bar chart 120-122
  creating 120
  crosstabs 122, 123
  density maps 147
  dual-axis chart 140
  filled maps 143
  highlight table 127, 128
  line charts 131-133
  point maps 144-146
  scatter plots 137, 138
  stacked bar chart 129

G

green field
  versus blue field 69-72

H

heat map 127

highlight table 127
  creating 127, 128
  insights 128, 129

histograms 171
  creating 171, 172
  visualization example 173

I

**International Components for
Unicode (ICU) 79**

J

joins
  basics 117

L

legends 194
  hiding 195
  moving 195
  re-applying 195
line charts 131
  creating 131-133
  insights 134
live data connection 94
  creating 96, 97
  versus extracted connections 94
live, versus extracted connections
  data recency 94
  offline work 95
  performance/speed 95
LOD expressions 86
  order of operations 87
  reference link 87
logical functions 81
  AND 81
  CASE 81
  ELSE 81
  ELSEIF 81
  END 81
  IF 81
  IFNULL 81
  IIF 81

ISNULL 81
MAX 81
MIN 81
OR 82
reference link 82
THEN 82

M

manual sorting
  managing 162
marks appearance
  managing 75, 76
  reference link 76
mark sizing 191
  advanced sizing options 193, 194
  basic sizing 192, 193
Marks section
  in Tableau 72, 73
mark types 73, 74

N

non-Tableau Server 9
noodles 105
number formatting
  reference link 40
number functions 78
  ABS 78
  MAX 78
  MIN 78
  reference link 79
  ZN 79
number note 69

O

one-chart data visualization 36
  example 37, 38
order of operations 88
  exclude 87
  fixed 87
  include 87
  reference link 88

P

parameters 88, 171
  reference link 88
pills 69
point map 144
  creating 144-146
  insights 147

Q

quantitative color marks 178, 179
  management 180, 181

R

reference lines 164
  adding 164
  considerations 167
  creating 164
  formatting 166
  instructions 164
  modifying 165

S

scatter plots 137
  creating 137, 138
  insights 139
sequential color marks 178
sets 157
  dynamic sets 160
  fixed sets 157, 158
shape marks
  Edit Shape field 188-190
  formatting 188
  reference link 74
Show Me charts 16-19
stacked bar chart 129, 176
  creating 129
  insights 131
story 217
  creating 217, 218
string functions 79
  LEFT 79
  LTRIM 80
  reference link 80
  RIGHT 79
  RTRIM 80
  SPLIT 79
  TRIM 79

T

Tableau 3
  filters and actions 46-55
  Marks section 72, 73
  mark types 73, 74
  order of operations 88
Tableau Desktop 6
  application basics 7
  certification 3, 4

certification for United Kingdom 6
certification for United States 5
dashboards 10
data connection 7-9
stories 10
worksheets 10
worksheet data pane 11
Tableau functions 78
basic aggregate functions 82
date functions 80
logical functions 81, 82
number functions 78
reference link 82
string functions 79
Tableau's data model 105, 106
Tableau Public application
download link 7
Tableau Server 8
table calculations 167
basic table calculation instructions 168
basic table calculations 167, 168
creating 168, 169
working with 170
text tables 122-127
Tooltip Editor 58
fonts, formatting 185-187
tooltips 57
default tooltips 57
insert actions 59

U

unions 28, 112, 113
considerations 116
creating 114, 115
wildcard (automatic) unions 115, 116

V

visualization animations
animation notes 191
configuring 190
configuring, for workbooks 191
visualization, formatting 176
colors, using from Marks card 176
fonts, configuring 181
legends, managing 194
mark sizing 191
shape marks, formatting 188
viz-in-tooltips 75

W

wildcard (automatic) unions 115, 116
workbook
sharing as file, on server 219, 220
underlying data, exporting 220
underlying data, viewing 220
viewing 218
worksheet data pane 11
columns 12
filters 14
marks 13, 14
quick measure adjustments 15, 16
rows 12
worksheet level formatting
reference link 44

Packtpub.com

Subscribe to our online digital library for full access to over 7,000 books and videos, as well as industry leading tools to help you plan your personal development and advance your career. For more information, please visit our website.

Why subscribe?

- Spend less time learning and more time coding with practical eBooks and Videos from over 4,000 industry professionals
- Improve your learning with Skill Plans built especially for you
- Get a free eBook or video every month
- Fully searchable for easy access to vital information
- Copy and paste, print, and bookmark content

Did you know that Packt offers eBook versions of every book published, with PDF and ePub files available? You can upgrade to the eBook version at packtpub.com and as a print book customer, you are entitled to a discount on the eBook copy. Get in touch with us at customercare@packtpub.com for more details.

At www.packtpub.com, you can also read a collection of free technical articles, sign up for a range of free newsletters, and receive exclusive discounts and offers on Packt books and eBooks.

Other Books You May Enjoy

If you enjoyed this book, you may be interested in these other books by Packt:

Data Modeling with Tableau

Kirk Munroe

ISBN: 978-1-80324-802-8

- Showcase Tableau published data sources and embedded connections
- Apply Ask Data in data cataloging and natural language query
- Understand the features of Tableau Prep Builder with the help of hands-on exercises
- Model data with Tableau Desktop using examples
- Formulate a governed data strategy using Tableau Server and Tableau Cloud
- Optimize data models for Ask and Explain Data

Microsoft Power BI Data Analyst Certification Guide

Orrin Edenfield, Edward Corcoran

ISBN: 978-1-80323-856-2

- Connect to and prepare data from a variety of sources
- Clean, transform, and shape your data for analysis
- Create data models that enable insight creation
- Analyze data using Microsoft Power BI's capabilities
- Create visualizations to make analysis easier
- Discover how to deploy and manage Microsoft Power BI assets

Packt is searching for authors like you

If you're interested in becoming an author for Packt, please visit authors.packtpub.com and apply today. We have worked with thousands of developers and tech professionals, just like you, to help them share their insight with the global tech community. You can make a general application, apply for a specific hot topic that we are recruiting an author for, or submit your own idea.

Share Your Thoughts

Now you've finished *Tableau Desktop Specialist Certification*, we'd love to hear your thoughts! Scan the QR code below to go straight to the Amazon review page for this book and share your feedback or leave a review on the site that you purchased it from.

https://packt.link/r/1-801-81013-3

Your review is important to us and the tech community and will help us make sure we're delivering excellent quality content.

Download a free PDF copy of this book

Thanks for purchasing this book!

Do you like to read on the go but are unable to carry your print books everywhere?

Is your eBook purchase not compatible with the device of your choice?

Don't worry, now with every Packt book you get a DRM-free PDF version of that book at no cost.

Read anywhere, any place, on any device. Search, copy, and paste code from your favorite technical books directly into your application.

The perks don't stop there, you can get exclusive access to discounts, newsletters, and great free content in your inbox daily

Follow these simple steps to get the benefits:

1. Scan the QR code or visit the link below

https://packt.link/free-ebook/9781801810135

2. Submit your proof of purchase
3. That's it! We'll send your free PDF and other benefits to your email directly

Made in the USA
Monee, IL
28 October 2023

45359027R00155